HARK!
The Biography of
Christmas

HARK!
The Biography of
Christmas

PAUL KERENSA

LION

Published by Lion Books
an imprint of
Lion Hudson IP Ltd
Wilkinson House, Jordan Hill Road,
Oxford OX2 8DR, England
www.lionhudson.com/lion

ISBN 978 0 7459 8017 1
e-ISBN 978 0 7459 8049 2

First edition 2017

Text acknowledgments
Scripture quotations from The Authorized (King James) Version. Rights in the
Authorized Version are vested in the Crown. Reproduced by permission of the
Crown's patentee, Cambridge University Press.

p. 223 Extract © Henry Williamson, reprinted by permission of Henry
Williamson Literary Estate.

Picture acknowledgments
Alamy: pp. 48, 148, 174, 128 Chronicle; p. 64 robertharding; p. 114 Michele
Castellani; p. 230 Heritage Image Partnership Ltd; p. 246 Moviestore

Superstock: p. 24 ACME Imagery; p. 88 Classic Vision / age fotostock; p. 160
ClassicStock.com; p. 210 World History Archive

A catalogue record for this book is available from the British Library

Printed and bound in the UK, August 2017, LH26

CONTENTS

For Mum & Dad
Thanks for all the stocking-fillers and turkey
Here's one for you
(A stocking-filler hopefully, not a turkey)

"Christmas time! That man must be a misanthrope indeed, in whose breast something like a jovial feeling is not roused."
Charles Dickens, *A Christmas Dinner*

"It's Chriiiiiistmas!"
Me, aged 8, singing along to *Top of the Pops*

Foreword

I love Paul Kerensa. Honestly, I do. I have actual love for the guy. The guy whose name, "Kerensa", actually translates as "love". Ancient Cornish and all that. Ah, yes, now that's another thing: Paul is actually from Cornwall. Which I also love. And he currently lives in Guildford, not too far away from my mum who I really, really, really love. Even more than Paul.

I work with Paul and have done for a good few years. Four, five, six, maybe more. I've never been a counter when it comes to jobs. It leads to desperate self-justification, quantity over quality, relevance, and most of all talent. Mmm… talent. Kerensa is overflowing with it. PK's scripts for our daily feature "Pause For Thought" on Radio 2 are nothing short of perfect. Their rhythm, their lightness of touch, his love of language, his wordplay, his understanding of people and the ever-crazier world which becomes ever more mind-meltingly difficult to make sense of each and every day, are evident for all to hear. And most annoyingly of all, he's very funny – but the real kicker is, he's such an incredibly nice guy. If I could steal anyone's warmth, and contentment, combined with the uncanny ability to care and comprehend enough to be able to convey much of what might otherwise go unnoticed to the rest of us, it would be a dead heat between Paul and Father Brian D'Arcy. (I've no time to tell you about Father Brian here, save to say, he's a living and breathing saint of a man, no miracles required. He is a walking miracle. No more genuine a human being has God's earth ever seen.)

And so what's Mr K up to here? He's only gone and written one of the most blindingly obvious behind-the-scenes stories thus far yet to be told. The truth about Christmas! Goodness me, why didn't I think of that? Like all the greatest comedy routines, it's been staring us in the face for decades. I adore Christmas, and having now read the following tinseltastic tome, I have years of festive pub ammo with which to regale my fellow merrymakers over however many Yuletides I have left.

Wait till you read about how paranoid Herod was that no one would be "sad enough" after he died, and what he ordered to be done about such posthumous injustice. Or how come "While Shepherds Watched Their Flocks" was the only Christmas carol that could be legally sung for over a century? Were The Three Kings really kings at all, and were there really three of them in the first place? Oh my giddy antlers, so many questions, but finally all the answers.

My favourite present under Paul's Christmas tree of literary wonder is the tale behind Charles Dickens' *A Christmas Carol* – my favourite book of all time. Always has been and always will be. How it came about. What it began as, compared to what it became. The personal risk Dickens took to get the book published at all. And my favourite part, the effect it had on countless real-life Scrooges back then and still today. Be prepared: there's so much to munch on.

This is a simply fabulous idea, and like all the best ideas it also happens to be fabulously simple.

Enjoy.

Oh, and a very merry Christmas.

Especially to you, PK – you truly deserve it.

Chris Evans

On my first page of Christmas...

'Twas the part before Prologue, and all through the pages,
Christmas was waiting, as it has through the ages...

Let nothing in the pages after this one sway you from this fact: I love Christmas. I love it quiet and candlelit, I love it loud and floodlit, I love its lessons, its carols, its ridiculous jumpers, and its turkey leftovers.

I also love history, though I've never studied it. But I have studied story. I adore anecdotes, quirks, and trivia, so expect plenty to litter what's to come. But I'll leave discovering the exact historical truth to the historians. I'm here to tell some stories. I'm a storian.

Whether your typical festivities are big and boisterous or sacred and solemn, I hope that you'll find your Christmas tucked away somewhere in this attic of a book. You just might have to move a few boxes of decorations to find it.

We'll visit Christmas' great turning-points and the origin of great innovations. Beyond the familiar tales of Scrooge and Santa, we'll hear about the lesser-known bizarre Christmas connections. Which broadcasting achievement was written by Englebert Humperdinck (not that one)? Which near-miss Gospel had the first use of the sci-fi concept of time standing still? Was St Nicholas the first to use an automatic door? How did Christmas change when the Reformation split churches from Rome (let's call it "Rexit"...)?

A confession: I am English, sorry (apology comes as standard with the nationality). I often glance this way to the Americas though, and that way to the Continent. So my particular focus on what has created the classic Christmas I know is based in Britain, but with plenty of visits from Uncle Sam, a glut of gifts from Mother Europe, and a few makeweights from Great Auntie Elsewhere. So that still means a more international story than any Bond film. We'll fly from Bethlehem to Cornwall, stopping at Scandinavia, Rome, Greece, Germany, Mexico, Japan, Russia, France, and maybe even Lapland. London will bring us feasting, Dickens, pantomime, and broadcasting grandeur. Our North American cousins will say goodbye to King George then "Happy Holidays" to George Washington, Washington Irving, and Irving Berlin (there was clearly a name shortage for a while).

As I see it, there are – how convenient – twelve key dates that helped shape the modern Christmas, so one by one we'll go through them (because you can't open all your presents at once). While we're there, we'll look at the era surrounding each date and the various stocking-fillers that history has offered us along the way, from Mary to Mariah Carey, candles to Handel, banned festivities to Band Aid.

Finally we'll reach our own Christmas, so that maybe next time you dust the snow off your Advent calendar, find a Cliff Richard CD in your Christmas pudding, or discover last year's turkey leg in your Christmas stocking*, you'll have a new appreciation of where it came from. A huge thank you to my wife for tolerating my obsession while making this book, and to my young children for throwing frequent festive facts at me. Thanks to Mum, Dad, and Mark for shaping my festive season over the years, and to grandparents gone for doing likewise – because of course Christmas is all about what's handed down to you. Thanks to my agents Nick Ranceford-Hadley and Greg Sammons; Simon Cox,

*Actually I can't help you with these.

Jessica Tinker, Drew Stanley, and all at Lion Hudson; James Cary for the Reformation checks; the Pilgrim Morris Men of Guildford for the mumming tips; and to Jon, Jen, Kat, and Sam of Onslow Christmas for unknowingly helping forge this idea, while we were larking about with retellings of "Ebenezer and Ivorezer Scrooge", that notorious Victorian double act.

So onward. I shall be your Ghost of Christmas Past – good evening – before we spend a bit of time with the Ghost of Christmas Present, and then approximately a paragraph with the Ghost of Christmas Future.

Ahead of our first date of Christmas though, we have history's Christmas Eve, which lasted several thousand years. And look there – for pretty much the only time in this book, I think it's going to snow…

Prologos: In the Bleak Midwinter

It's been said that Christmas starts with Christ. I agree, but – thousands of years before the Nativity stable – Christmas had an ancestor.

Like many aged relatives during the festive season, this ancestor stoically returned year on year, stayed for a few days, and bestowed stories and food down the generations. The storytelling helped this pre-Christmas "Christmas" endure for thousands of years; in many respects its descendants are still with us today.

A familiar lament is what a non-Christian Christmas looks like. If it's a festival in the dead of winter gathering family, friends, and neighbours to gorge on shared meals, with fires lit and gifts given – then this is it. There might be dressing up and a bit of a dance, familiar traditions wheeled out for another year, against a backdrop of evergreens like holly and ivy.

This could describe a secular Christmas today or 6,000 years ago. Thousands of years before the Nativity of Jesus, the party wasn't to remember the Bethlehem boy, but to urge on spring – not praising the Risen Son, but praising the Rising Sun.

It began before the little town of Bethlehem, and in fact before any town. Back then, all this was just fields – and we'd only just worked out how to farm them.

CHRISTMAS IS PLANTED

The invention of agriculture sowed the seeds of a midwinter festival. Before we settled into villages and towns, we learned to toil the land. Hunter-gathering gave way to this new concept of farming. Crops could be grown in a fraction of the space normally plundered by hunters for fruit, vegetables, or meat.

Farming took root independently across the world, as different civilizations discovered how to tame the land. But the first to master it? The inhabitants of the Fertile Crescent, from today's Jordan and Israel to Iraq, via Syria and Turkey. So for those who like to think that the roots of Christmas lie in the Holy Land – good news, they do indeed.

The farmland of the Middle East was as good as it gets, housing over half of the world's edible grass types (Western Europe, by contrast, could only produce the simple oat). It's here that around 13,000 years ago, the last ice age defrosted the Earth's great larder – and we learned how to raid it. But like all larder raids, sometimes you take too much, and for the first time we discovered what a food surplus looked like. Especially in the icy north, holding back superfluous food became a must for winter survival.

It would take at least 5,000 years for agriculture to reach all corners of Europe. It's apt for the story of Christmas that farming began in the Middle East, with the Scandinavians being the last continental Europeans to discover it. Our tale will ping back and forth within this zone several times, via the Mediterranean and the Germanic north. We'll return to the Fertile Crescent soon enough, for some rather miraculous springtime fertility, but first let's spend winter in Scandinavia.

A STORY OF ICE AND FIRE

Winter was coming, and its bite was fierce; Northern Europeans knew more than most that for a hope of a gnaw on anything during the coldest months, canny food storage was key. Unfortunately, they didn't have cans.

Farming was imported north by southern European immigrants gradually, over generations. A 2012 study of genetics, led by Mattias Jakobsson at Uppsala University, confirmed that Scandinavia became the endpoint of agriculture's European travels, as if blocked by a wall of ice. By around 4000–3000 BC, these incoming farmers mixed with local hunter-gatherers, working side by side.

The locals learned how to farm, although due to the tilt of the northern hemisphere away from the sun, very little agricultural work could be achieved during winter. The arrival of farming also meant more mouths to feed. Hunter-gatherers could only have as many children as they could carry, but farmland meant a homeland, and a bumper crop of children.

To fend off the icy north's unique challenges, consumption was deliberately rationed and food stored. But not all of it could be stored for long, so winter's midpoint became the perfect time to bring out some of these stored goods, partly through necessity, but also because it's good to pop a cork when the worst is over.

Specialist farming meant that different families grew different foodstuffs, so food-swapping became a sensible strategy to give a varied diet. Edible exchanges meant not just a meal but a midwinter feast for everyone, each year on the winter solstice – "solstice" meaning "sun stands still".

But one thing that wasn't a given was the fact the sun would come back. The return of spring, and afterwards the crops, could not be presumed, so sun worship became a key part of the celebration. Since ancient days, the sun had been worshipped, giving the midwinter feast a spiritual dimension, with rituals to encourage the sun's return. By celebrating on the shortest day, the leaders were confident that the days *should* lengthen from there, so any worship would be mystically rewarded with more daylight before long.

Fire was a crucial part of the rituals; after all, to make fire was to visibly recreate the sun on earth. A wheel of fire, representing the sun, would be rolled into the sea, and some fires would burn for days on end to show defiance of nature.

These rituals were mankind's way of jumpstarting nature back into life. The unique geography and living challenges created an annual event that became core to the local Norse culture: a festival called Yule.

YULE BURNER

No one knows when Yule began, but it's one of the most ancient festivals on our planet: a pagan celebration spanning three nights at midwinter. At its heart was feasting, and the notion of fire amid frost – seemingly miraculous back then, still echoed today in our captivation with winter bonfires. To burn constantly through the season, there was a lot of pressure (and therefore significance) placed on the Yule log. It represented health and fertility, the concept of life persisting when nature is against you.

The Yule log is a direct ancestor of our Christmas tree, and just like today, sourcing and retrieving it would be a seasonal errand in itself. Once sourced, the log would be doused with wine so it could burn for days, then placed at the centre of festivities – so you could see what was going on if nothing else.

When the sun returned, the season ended and the log's work was done. But a fragment would be kept for use the next year. Continuity was everything, forging a link to the past and ensuring the future of the festival, similar to our Christmas traditions today. (Can you imagine binning *all* of your Christmas decorations and starting again from scratch? Ugh.) Through the year, the log's ashes also had a role to play, scattered through the fields to give fertile crops, or sprinkled into wells to purify the water (though it might make you cough).

Four Yuletide customs...

✧ *EAT!...* Where there was fire, there would be sacrifices: livestock were slain and their sacrificial blood, *hlaut*, was daubed over people and idols in tribute to the Norse gods. The meat was blessed and then eaten (no food could be wasted in this harsh, wintry climate).

✧ *DRINK!...* Ale was raised to the king, to departed ancestors, and to the gods Odin (or Woden), Thor, Freyr, and Njörðr. Those gods, as you may have guessed, gave us some of our days of the week: Wednesday, Thursday, Friday, and Njörðrsday – alright, Njörðrsday never caught on, but I like to think it's that extra sliver of time you wish you had between Sunday and Monday...

✧ *BE... AFRAID*, be very afraid. The honouring of dead ancestors became a major theme of the festival. It was said they'd return at Yule, in a "Yule hunt" of the living. Woe betide any youngster who ventured out on their own at this time of year! To this day, a Finnish Christmas might include a candlelit family trip to the graves of ancestors. Some Finns still spend Christmas night sleeping on the floor – for one night a year, the beds are left for the ghosts of their departed relatives.

✧ *MERRY!...* There was lighter pretence in a midwinter play: a man would dress up as "Winter", a forerunner of Father Christmas and Santa Claus. Similar to the Nativity plays we're now used to, it was part community fun, part theological origin story. Others would wear horse-head masks, animal skins, or reindeer antlers. And speaking of reindeer... ah, we'll get to them later.

IT'S NOT EASY BEING EVERGREEN

From animals to evergreens, nature was at the root of the Yule customs. Plants that grew year-round, such as holly, ivy, and mistletoe, became popular adornments for the home, their rebellion against the season giving the impression of special powers of fertility.

The holly represented the male (it was something to do with the berries) and the ivy the female. The plant hung on the doorway theoretically governed which gender might rule the house that year. Growing between ground and sky, these evergreens were said to link mankind to the heavens. Holly's sharp edges gave it some extra evil-repelling significance too (even evil hates being pricked by shrubbery, which may be why so many supervillains wear gloves).

The church has fallen in and out of love with this evergreenery over the years. The plants were banned for some time, so they became simple decorations purely for the home. At other times Christianity has claimed holly back again, the thorns representing Christ's crown of thorns and the red berries his blood. To this day, the Danish word for holly is "*kristtjørn*" – "Christ thorn".

In the secular world too, fashions for evergreens have blossomed and faded; the Anglo-Saxons called mistletoe "dung on a twig", thanks to the mistle thrush's habit of eating the berries and excreting them, so more mistletoe would grow in its place – a sign of fertility perhaps, if a grubby one.

FROM NORTH TO SOUTH

Other aspects of ancient Yule have persisted through the ages, if only in Scandinavia. The figure of the Yule goat, for example, was based on the goats said to pull Thor's chariot, embodying those familiar Norse themes of sacrifice and fertility. For centuries after, Scandinavian men dressed up in goatskins to sing songs at each house, like the carolling and wassailing we'll find elsewhere in Europe. Swedes might enact the *Juleoffer*, a performance of "Yule sacrifice" where folks dress up and "slay" the Yule goat, who would "die" then return to life.

Yule developed from an essential exercise in winter food-sharing into a rite deep with meaning. But although its entire purpose was to return the sunlight, a lightness was perhaps what was missing. As a festival it remained dark, fixated on the death of ancestors and fighting against the death of nature. Winter had come, and these kings in the north had diligently kept watch over this festival for generations. For Yule to become Christmas though, winter would have to give way to the coming of spring – new life and new light, personified by Jesus, Christians' "light of the world".

The names "Yule" and "Christmas" may be almost synonymous today, but they are wholly distinct occasions. Yule was an event of its own, lasting down the millennia far longer than Christmas has. While the party continued in the north, it certainly cleared a path for new celebrations in the south, handing over the reins to its Christian counterpart.

Many books have a prologue but ours is "*pro logos*" – Greek for "before The Word". The evangelist John calls Jesus the pre-existent "*logos*" in the opening of his Gospel, the Word who became flesh and dwelled among mankind. The Norse folk thought that evergreens were the bridge between heaven and earth, but for Christians, God meets man in a Bethlehem shack.

While Scandinavia was moving, later than most, from Stone Age into Bronze Age, 3,000 miles away the Israelites were wandering the wilderness, puzzling out what it meant to have one God instead of several. Monotheism was a new idea at that time. And 1,000 years after that, another new theological concept was born with Christianity, summed up in a name: Immanuel, "God with us". To this grand mess of festivity, we add Christ, to become Christmas.

Nativity by Gerard David (1455–1523),
oil on wood, early 1480s

Chapter 1

The First Nowell

(4 BC–AD 300)

Christmas is no twin of Jesus. It didn't arrive fully formed as a festival, and it certainly wasn't born on 25 December AD 0. Then again, neither was Jesus.

Throughout history, Christmas has behaved more like one of its own evergreen trees, blossoming when least expected and showing surprising resilience in tough times. As we've seen, the notion of a midwinter festival took root before Christ, and it would grow a long time after, though many would try to cut it down before its prime – and even the church would come to wield that axe at times. But the buds of Christmas did burst through the ground where we might expect, in the fields of turn-of-the-millennium Palestine, on the eastern edge of the Roman empire.

Like Rome, Christmas wasn't built in a day – but we must zoom in on that one day, the first Nowell. In this chapter we'll look afresh at the Nativity and its attendants, and we'll see how those early origin stories don't always offer what we might assume: we won't find an inn but we might find the odd talking animal. We'll also drop in on four school Nativity plays: at St Matthew's, St Mark's, St Luke's, and St John's.

A RIGHT ROYAL THREAT

By the time of the Nativity, Roman rule had endured and expanded, conquering many different peoples and cultures. They were absorbed as Roman reach grew, so for the most part worship was permitted of whatever gods the locals preferred, as long as they didn't mind joining in with some Roman worship too.

With Judaism though, the Romans stumbled into a problem. Here for the first time was a monotheistic religion, worshipping just one God, with no room for worship of Roman gods and eventually the emperor. Attempting to govern the Jews was therefore tricky, with various systems tried from tolerance to ghettoization. The Roman republic being so vast at that time meant that delegating to local governors seemed best, "client kings" ruling on behalf of Rome.

One of these was the Jewish-raised Herod the Great, a fierce tyrant ever ready to quash dissent. After all, Rome had decreed him "King of the Jews" in 40 BC. No one was going to take that title away from him – especially not a baby...

Seven highlights from Herod's curriculum vitae...

✧ *SECRET OF SUCCESS...* Herod prospered thanks to fierce ambition, ruthless tyranny, and his swift and fickle change of allegiance to whoever was Rome's winning side.

✧ *MARRY ME, MARIAMNE...* Herod had ten wives (not all at the same time), including a Cleopatra and two Mariamnes. His first wife had the earthier name of Doris.

✧ *BIG SPENDER...* Herod was noted for rash spending, trying to win favour by ordering huge building projects, from harbours to fortresses to the Second Temple. The locals didn't buy it though, largely because he was also busy...

✧ *KILLING PEOPLE...* The execution of all Bethlehem boys under two, known as the Massacre of the Innocents, is in the Scriptures but not the history books of the time. It's entirely likely though, in keeping with a tyrant who killed anyone in his way, including three of his own sons. He drowned his teenage brother-in-law at a party, and once made his mother-in-law testify against his wife, her daughter – before killing them both.

✧ *THE INNOCENTS…* The massacre has been estimated at no more than twenty boys, since the order was gender-, age-, and location-specific; Bethlehem was little more than a village. It's still awful, mind you.

✧ *SAFETY IN NUMBERS…* If you ever wondered why no one killed him off, Herod had 2,000 bodyguards.

✧ *MISS ME?…* The threat didn't vanish when he died. Herod was gravely paranoid, and feared that he wouldn't be mourned. So he ordered the mass executions of various distinguished and well-liked citizens, to take place between his death and funeral. That way his people would have something to cry about. Thankfully his next of kin chose not to carry out this wish. Herod died of kidney disease and gangrene – reportedly an excruciating exit.

IT'S A DATE!

We don't know exactly when Jesus was born, but it wasn't AD 0, because there was no AD 0. The dating system, created centuries later and applied retrospectively, has it jumping from 1 BC to AD 1. Either way, historians of all creeds and none acknowledge that there was a Jesus, and though we might argue over his death and what came after, we can agree that there was a date and place of birth. We can place the "where" as Bethlehem, but the "when" has been a very movable feast, spanning around a decade.

Herod died in 4 BC, so that would place Jesus' birth earlier than that. But Quirinius, Governor of Syria mentioned in Luke's Gospel, didn't take office until AD 6 according to the historian Josephus, who also tells us there was a census at the same time. Add into the puzzle the star factor – a bright one could be tracked to perhaps 6 BC.

As for the time of the year – well, if the Norse Yule seemed dark and wintry, now we have probably a spring birth. It's doubtful that Jesus was born in midwinter, let alone on 25 December. Spring is a more suitable time of year for a census check, as well as for the presence of lambs in fields, and for watching those flocks by night. After the frosty foundations of Christmas' Scandinavian ancestor, new life prospers here in warmer climes, in warmer months.

Clement of Alexandria in AD 200 suggested 20 May or 20 or 21 April; others suggested 21 or 28 March, or 2 April. Over the centuries, various calculations have been attempted, working back from Jesus' adult ministry or supposed death date, or working forward from John the Baptist's supposed conception at the autumn equinox. The truth is that we can't know.

Perhaps it's irrelevant anyway, about as useful as knowing Jesus' shoe size. The fine biographical details are not the issue; what matters for our story of Christmas (and indeed for the Christian faith at large) is that he was born, and what came after. Just as the Genesis creation account is best read as poetry and theology rather than history, so do the Nativity accounts offer more when read as an origin story, rather than a biographical entry in *Who's Who*.

ADAM II: THIS TIME IT'S PERSONAL

If it was a spring birth, how have we ended up with a midwinter Christmas? In chapter 2 we'll see how other Roman festivals may have helped guide the church to this particular date three centuries later, but the church latched onto other reasons for 25 December.

The chief theories rely on 25 March being the day of Angel Gabriel's visit to Mary, meaning that's the date of Jesus' conception in her womb: the Annunciation. Nine months from this date brings us to 25 December – because if anyone's going to be born bang on their due date, it's the Messiah.

So why the 25 March conception date? One tradition held that Jewish prophets had an "integral age": their purity meant a lifespan of exact years, so their dates of conception (or perhaps birth) and death were on the same date, with fully rounded years in between. I don't know if the prophets would have known this, in which case it would have made them rather nervous approaching their birthday each year. Other historical figures with the same birthday and deathday include Ingrid Bergman, Franklin D. Roosevelt, and Shakespeare – read into that what you will.

Tertullian of Carthage, writing two centuries post-Christ, calculated that a crucifixion date of the fourteenth of Nisan (as in John's Gospel) equalled 25 March in the Roman calendar. So if Jesus died on 25 March, then his integral age would mean a birth or conception of 25 March. If the latter, that gives a 25 December birthday.

A second theory is based on Jesus' role as "the New Adam", born to redeem the sin and mess started by the first Adam. Creation, the Garden of Eden, and Adam himself were all linked to the first day of spring – and would you Adam and Eve it, that was thought to be 25 March.

By the time these theories had proliferated, 25 December was already a popular time to celebrate Jesus' birth, so perhaps these were retrofitted. Whatever the reason for the celebration date, whenever Jesus was actually born, we can piece together a few details of that first Nowell, thanks to the gospel writers Matthew and Luke:

On our first date of Christmas…
(Bethlehem, approximately 20 May 4 BC)
After a week-long journey, Mary finally rests.

For generations, her ancestors have trusted in a prophecy: their dynasty – the family line of Jesse – would produce a new King of the Jews. Perhaps this king would free the tyrannized Israelites, ushering in a new age with renewed hope for a holy Jewish nation. King David belonged to that family line, so his town of Bethlehem was foretold as this revolutionary leader's birthplace.

In quiet days of their youth, Mary's mother and her mother before her wondered if they would be the one to carry this child. For this Galilee peasant woman, it's true; she's virginal, yet as an angel appeared to her, her womb filled. She knows the weight of this journey from Nazareth: privately it fulfils the prophecy, but publicly it fulfils the government demand for a census.

Travelling with her husband Joseph, the ninety-mile trip has not been easy while so heavily pregnant. They've crossed mountains and hiked rough tracks past olive groves, joining with other travellers through Judea's barren wilderness to stay safe, to avoid bears or bandits (their son will one day tell of an injured traveller on this road, helped by a good Samaritan). They've stayed with friendly Jewish households or in small camps, in more comfortable conditions than journey's end now provides.

The census means that many others of Jesse's line have converged on Bethlehem too, so lodging is hard to come by. They have little more than a cave, but it's shelter at least, and an animal's feeding-trough provides somewhere to lay the baby.

The night is not silent. Mary labours in this temporary shelter, open to animals and the elements. Yet here, the baby is born and named "Yeshua" in Hebrew, or "Jesus" in Greek, meaning "Saviour" or "salvation of the Lord".

Angels send shepherds to bow down and greet the child. Much later, a bright star will guide wise men, mystics known as Magi, from the eastern plains. They'll offer gifts and worship the boy, but as itinerant mystics they'll also draw the attention of King Herod, which means danger. The baby's family will flee to Egypt for safety – but that's for another day.

Today's news is simply this: Mary the virgin has given birth to a baby boy, now resting in a manger.

CAVE MARIA

That one final sentence is about all that can be agreed on in the two Gospels that report Jesus' birth.

The world's greatest festival is unfortunately recounted only briefly and in just Matthew and Luke, two of the four Gospels; Mark instead begins with a genealogy, while John presents a poetic spiritual prologue. Matthew and Luke's Nativity accounts have elements in common, but most familiar details, from shepherd to census to frankincense, only feature in one of them.

Is this problematic for Christianity? Perhaps; this key event is at best underreported, so much hanging on just twenty verses in each of Matthew and Luke's Gospels (Matthew 1:18–2:12; Luke 2:1–20). Then again, the lack of information could be seen to help narrow the focus. If all the two Nativity Gospels can agree on is the miraculous lowly birth, then maybe that's what matters to the Christian faith.

And it was lowly. We may think of a stable, but we're never told that there was one, just that there was a manger – and in their agricultural society, feeding-troughs were on the street or in makeshift shelters. In AD 135, Emperor Hadrian is said to have converted the cave into a shrine for the Greek god Adonis, a grove was planted to wipe away Christian worship, and around the same time early Christian writer Justin Martyr writes of a specific cave in which Jesus was born. The significance of this simple shelter was clearly well-known.

Mary and Joseph were certainly poor too. We're told that in thanks for Jesus' birth, they offered the peasants' sacrifice, of "a pair of turtledoves, or two young pigeons" (Luke 2:24 KJV) as opposed to a lamb. These impoverished beginnings have been crucial for Christianity, allying Jesus to the cause of the poor over the centuries. But while the church's message has dwelled on the poverty, church doctrine has fixated on Mary's virginity.

THE IMMACULATE MISCONCEPTION

The virgin birth is not to be confused with the immaculate conception. Ask any non-Catholic the question of who was immaculately conceived, and they'll probably say Jesus, in Mary's womb. Zero points. It refers to Mary, conceived as standard via human mother and father, but divinely redeemed at the moment of her conception. The Catholic belief is that original sin, handed down to the rest of us ever since Adam, skipped Mary. This meant that when *she* conceived Jesus, in the *virginal conception*, she had no sin to pass onto him – and obviously Jesus' heavenly Father didn't pass any down either. So Jesus was not the subject of the immaculate conception… but it's a common misconception.

The virginal conception brings its own paradox – but then again, that's the idea. Theologians have actually pondered whether Mary's hymen remained intact during Jesus' birth (Catholic teaching thinks yes), though perhaps such questions miss the point. The eleventh-century Abbot of Westminster Gilbert Crispin suggested that Christ's birth was like sunlight passing through a pane of glass: morning may have broken, but nothing else has. Some medieval depictions of Jesus' conception showed him travelling from heaven to Mary, not entering via womb but through her ear. The moment of conception was surely when Mary heard the news from the Angel Gabriel – but perhaps you, like me, read this thinking such solutions are a bit too specific. If we're asking biological answers of Mary, perhaps we're asking the wrong person the wrong questions. Whether or not miracles exist, their place in storytelling is to mystify, rather than make us puzzle out a workaround.

MARY, QUITE CONTRARY?

The virgin birth is perhaps taken for granted today: presumed true by Christians, presumed wrong by sceptics, uttered and muttered in the church creeds as a core tenet of faith. This strand of belief is a major supernatural leap, and one held by Islam too. Yet it wasn't widely accepted by Christianity until the second century, when the gospel accounts became more widely known and distributed. In these new Scriptures, Matthew's Gospel affirmed the miraculous status of the virgin birth, quoting Isaiah's prophecy from the Old Testament: "The Lord himself shall give you a sign; Behold, a virgin shall conceive, and bear a son, and shall call his name Immanuel" (7:14 KJV).

There have been dissenting voices though. Isaiah's Hebrew word for "virgin" – *almah* – could also translate as "young woman", in which case Isaiah's prophecy may not suggest a virgin birth. Regardless, Matthew deliberately champions a virgin birth, perhaps reframing Isaiah's prophecy to tell the story that he wants to tell. But then each Gospel is a portrait of Jesus from a different angle, highlighting different facets as the author wishes.

Matthew wrote before Christianity even existed, before the religion ran with his ideas. Catholicism especially saw Mary all through the Bible: as the woman spoken of in the Garden of Eden, as "the Daughter of Zion" depicted by Old Testament prophets, and as the "bride" in the Song of Solomon, thought by Protestants to be not Mary, but the church.

This "Mariology" (nothing to do with Nintendo) only grew through the Middle Ages. So while the sixteenth-century Reformation was more concerned with the Catholic selling of "indulgences" (pieces of paper that wrote off your sin for a fee), "the cult of Mary" didn't escape unscathed. But although the reformers downgraded Mary, it was only to elevate her son. Martin Luther, the first Protestant, noted that "we have an obligation to honour Mary – but be careful to give her honour that is fitting." From Luther to Calvin, they continued to champion the virgin birth.

Nine Choirs of Angels...

From the fourth century onwards, angels were thought to have three Hierarchies or Spheres, each containing three Choirs. It's not biblical, but – well, a great deal of time and thought has gone into it, and that should count for something.

- ✧ *SERAPHIM*… are top-flight angels, said to surround God's throne, constantly singing praises. They have three pairs of wings – one for flying, one to cover their feet, one to cover their faces, like celestial peekaboo.

- ✧ *CHERUBIM*… are said to guard the Garden of Eden. Ignore the chubby child-like cherubs in art (more correctly called "putti") – proper cherubim actually have four faces.

- ✧ *THRONES*… are angels resembling elderly men, who petition God with mankind's prayers.

✧ *DOMINIONS*… delegate to lower angelic ranks, and like others in the second Sphere are governors of creation.

✧ *VIRTUES*… are doers, enabling miracles.

✧ *POWERS*… oversee the cosmos, oppose evil spirits, and keep history in order. The latter makes them sound a bit like the angelic equivalent of Bill and Ted, marshalling Napoleon and Socrates from a shopping mall.

✧ *PRINCIPALITIES*… are a largely administrative role, particularly guiding nations or institutions.

✧ *ARCHANGELS*… The penultimate rank contains seven archangels, including Michael – the only angel other than Gabriel to be named in the Bible, when he visits Daniel. Alright, there's also Lucifer, but he's a fallen one, so we'll follow heaven's example and exclude him.

✧ *ANGELS*… The lowest rank, yet the most familiar. This is technically where Gabriel resides, though he's often considered an archangel. Gabriel first appears not to Mary but to Daniel in the Old Testament. St Augustine taught that "angel" was not a description of one's nature, but a job title: these are "messengers of God". While many think of angels as feminine, the only named biblical angels are male. Then there's the Angel of the North – that looks male. And the Angel Islington… which is blue in Monopoly.

FOUR NATIVITIES

From angels to angles, and four different ones from four Gospel-writers of different standpoints, with distinct audiences. Mark wrote first but has no Christmas story. Luke wrote next, for the Greek and Roman world, focusing on Mary. He starts in Nazareth and tells of the Angel Gabriel visiting Mary, as well as Mary's visit to her cousin Elizabeth. Matthew wrote for a Jewish audience, and focuses on Joseph. He starts in Bethlehem and tells of an angel visiting Joseph and of Herod's Massacre of the Innocents. Luke writes of shepherds; Matthew writes of wise men. John writes last and, like Mark, is *sans Noël*.

These are not contrasting timelines, but unique portraits. To see how each Gospel reports the details of that first Christmas, let's journey to four primary schools: St Matthew's, St Mark's, St Luke's, and St John's. Each has an annual Nativity play, but each is strictly tied to its own Gospel. They make for four very different performances…

ST MATTHEW'S INFANT SCHOOL NATIVITY PLAY

It's a thriller. Our play opens with a giant family tree, possibly read out by a child narrator, or better yet, projected as scrolling text on the big screen, like the opening to *Star Wars*: "A long time ago, in a land far away, Abraham was the father of Isaac, who was father of Jacob, who was father of…" Make it dramatic; show the backstory.

When it's rolled, we cut to Joseph having a troubled night's sleep. He's engaged to Mary, but he's just found out that she's pregnant, so he's going to divorce her – until a mid-dream angelic vision talks him out of it. This son is going to save people. Epic dramatic music to end the scene. St Matthew's Infant School has Hollywood production values.

(The schoolgirl dressed up to play Mary will at this point be waiting in the wings, eager to take the stage… But there's no angelic visitation for her at St Matthew's, alas.)

Mary gives birth, practically offstage. It's Joseph, instructed by the angel, who names the child Jesus. Father and son take centre-stage. Just as our rolling text showed fathers handing down to sons, so too does Joseph hand the limelight to Jesus – but it's still up to Joseph to protect him.

New scene, new location: Jerusalem, probably a year later. Evil King Herod hears that a group of travelling astrologers have come to town, tracking a star to find a "king of the Jews". The conniving king asks the astrologers to report back to him, so he can "worship" the king too. But does he mean the baby harm?

The astrologers track that star and pack gifts for the young king. The star comes to rest over a house, where they find Mary and her now toddler son Jesus.

Herod awaits news; the boy Jesus is under threat of death. The tension mounts. Will the wise men return to Herod and jeopardize the holy family? No, because they're wise. A vision tells them to return home another way.

Later still, there's another vision, this time to heroic Joseph: take your family and hide in Egypt. Sure enough, Herod sends troops to wipe out the boys. (This scene may be unsuitable for the Infant School – be sure to send around a note.) The holy family wait out the extermination, and when they do return, they lie low: Herod's successor seems just as dangerous.

St Matthew's play is an international chase thriller, against a backdrop of fulfilled prophecy and dreamed warnings. It's a tense, gory, male-focused biographical adventure; this school Nativity has very few roles for girls, although there's a genealogical prologue which does feature women in Jesus' family line, unusual for the patrilineal society of the day.

The St Matthew's props cupboard is unencumbered by a manger or stable. And any parents who've dressed their little ones as innkeepers, shepherds, or oxen – St Matthew's apologizes but they won't be gracing the stage, so cameras down. Mary too has no lines and hardly appears onstage. St Matthew's is, more than likely, an all-boys school.

THE ST MARK'S JUNIOR SCHOOL CHRISTMAS PLAY

…has been indefinitely cancelled. Instead there'll be a baptism. Don't sit in the front row unless you expect to get wet.

St Mark's Gospel begins with John the Baptist commissioning Jesus' ministry. Jesus is a grown man. Parents: put away the dressing-gowns and tea towels. The children at St Mark's School don't get a Nativity play.

THE NATIVITY PLAY OF ST LUKE'S CHURCH OF ENGLAND ACADEMY

St Luke's performance is the longest – and perhaps the most familiar – of the Nativity stories. Parents will be delighted that their little angel has been cast as, well, an angel, or perhaps a shepherd, or a lamb, or Theophilus. Who now? He's in the prologue, being told the story by Luke. And there are more unfamiliar characters: before we meet our favourites, there's the elderly childless couple Zechariah and Elizabeth. Zechariah's a priest at the temple, the first in the play to meet the Angel Gabriel. Gabriel tells Zechariah to expect a son, John, who will prepare people for the Lord. Zechariah doubts, so is struck dumb till the birth.

Scene two. The Angel Gabriel now visits Mary, Elizabeth's cousin, with news of her virgin birth to a boy called Jesus, Son of the Most High. Mary stays with Elizabeth, and Elizabeth's baby John leaps in her womb. John is born and Zechariah speaks again.

Caesar Augustus demands a census, so everyone treks to their home towns – that's Nazareth to Bethlehem for our star family. Mary gives birth to a boy! She wraps him in cloths and places him in a manger, because there's no room at the lodgings. Still no innkeeper onstage – sorry parents.

An angel appears to shepherds nearby, who hurry to the manger and spread word of the baby's arrival. On the eighth day, the boy is circumcised and named Jesus. They might cut this bit. I mean the scene, not… it's not suitable for a kids' Nativity, that's what I'm saying.

St Luke's has that natural ending of any school play: Joseph and Mary sacrifice two young pigeons, then they meet a righteous man called Simeon, who was promised he'd see Christ before he died, and an elderly prophetess called Anna.

The end! St Luke's bumper cast, take a bow.

ST JOHN'S PRIMARY SCHOOL NATIVITY PRESENTATION

Rather than a play, St John's presents an evening of poetry with interpretative dance. Children dressed as Joseph, Mary, angels, wise men, shepherds, and so on do not take the stage; they stay in the converted classroom-slash-dressing-room. Then again, they're not the star of the show. Even the star isn't the star of this show.

NO INN AT THE INN

There are some notable absences. Luke's Greek word "*kataluma*" is often translated "inn", but may be more "guest room": a spare room in Joseph's relative's home that was unsurprisingly full (well it *was* Christmas). So there wasn't just no room at the inn – there was no inn, and no room in the room. And is it just me that hears the grown-up Jesus later proclaim, "My Father's house has many rooms" and detects a knowing reference to the lack of accommodation thirty years previously? Yes, it is just me. Fair enough.

Whether innkeeper, shepherd, or donkey, they are all merely wrapping paper as far as Christians are concerned – the present is in the manger. Over the history of Christmas, we'll see layer upon layer added, from Santa to Scrooge to snow, but they start here in Bethlehem. These characters might be beloved of Nativity plays, but the gospel writers couldn't agree on them, and they remain bit parts.

LITTLE-MENTIONED DONKEY

The donkey isn't even a bit part – he's simply not there. All four Gospels record Jesus riding a donkey at the end of his life, for his triumphal entry into Jerusalem on Palm Sunday. It seems apt then that his entrance to the world might be heralded by a donkey. The humble animal even has a literal cross on its back in the shape of its hair, so in terms of narrative foreshadowing, the beast is a perfect fit for the Bethlehem trek.

Yet putting the donkey at our Nativity scene is to put the cart before the horse – and right there we have two other modes of transport Mary might have used. Horses were a grander travelling choice, not necessarily the reserve of the rich, but perhaps too attention-seeking for travellers after a lower profile. It may have been a donkey, it's a logical choice – the writers just don't tell us.

So apologies to the thousands of schoolchildren cast as that donkey each year in Nativity plays. Even Pope Benedict XVI saw fit to address this vital issue, writing in his 2012 book *Jesus of Nazareth: The Infancy Narratives*: "In the gospels there is no mention of animals." Perhaps British schools cling to the beloved beast partly thanks to the sentiment of children's carol "Little Donkey" – though even this is more recent than many realize. The song was written in 1959 by Eric Boswell, a folk musician from the northeast of England. He was actually prouder of his other more humorous animal songs, including "I've Got A Daft Pigeon" and "I've Got A Little Whippet".

Six biblical shepherds...

✧ *ABEL...* The Bible's first shepherd – and first murder victim. Mankind has been shepherding for 7,000 years, ever since we discovered, well, sheep. Before that we just stood around empty pens whistling at dogs for no real reason.

✧ *ABRAHAM...* sought land, sheep, and a relationship with God. Granted all three at a ripe old age.

✧ *DAVID...* started young, and went from shepherd boy to giant killer to king. Top that CV.

✧ *THE LORD...* is my shepherd, according to Psalm 23. Jesus later calls himself "The Good Shepherd", and passes his flock on to Peter, requesting: "Feed my sheep."

✧ *PRIESTS...* are therefore thought of as shepherds; "pastor" is Latin for "shepherd". Congregations are "flocks", and many priests wield that big crook (though rarely have to use it to wrangle a church-member).

✧ *EWE HERD...* As for our Nativity shepherds, the angelic greeting they received has become the motto for the season: "Peace on earth, good will to men". Even Linus in *A Charlie Brown Christmas* thinks these words sum up Christmas. Along with the Magi, their presence indicates a Messiah here for all, from poor Jewish field worker to distinguished gentile foreigner.

WISE GUYS

The three kings followed the star and gathered around the manger with the shepherds... didn't they?

There are several things wrong with that picture, though one probable accuracy is the star, likely to have been a conjunction of Saturn and Jupiter a few years BC. As for the visitors themselves, they were "Magi", probably followers of the Zoroastrian religion, possibly practitioners of magic, and certainly astrologers. The singular "Magus" is later applied to Simon Magus in the book of Acts, though Simon's use of sorcery is highly criticized – not a very wise man.

It's fair to say that they weren't kings and there weren't necessarily three of them; we're only told that they brought three gifts. There could have been two, with one carrying two gifts. There could have been more than three, some arriving empty-handed (the Syriac tradition suggests twelve Magi). From around AD 500 they gained names – Melchior, Caspar, and Balthazar – which only encouraged the idea of three of them. Around the same time, they shifted from being wise men to being kings, stemming from Old Testament prophecies that "kings shall fall down before him" (Psalm 72:11 KJV). Possibly, but not these kings. Because they weren't kings.

The rank and quantity of the deliverers are perhaps not as significant as their gifts. Frankincense is a sweet-smelling remedy for ailments from leprosy to mosquito bites, its scent representing life. Myrrh symbolizes death to come: it's an embalming resin named after the Greek god Myrrha, who was said to shed myrrh as tears – similar to a Christmas character we'll meet in 300 years, St Nicholas. And gold held great value then as today, fit for a king.

As to when these non-Jews visited the "king of the Jews", it was months or even years after Jesus' birth. They visit not the manger, stable, or cave, but Mary's house, and Joseph is not mentioned – paternity leave over.

There's further evidence in the Presentation at the Temple in Luke's Gospel, forty days after Jesus' birth. If the Magi warned the holy family to flee to Egypt, that implies that their arrival was later than the Temple visit; you wouldn't flee via a Temple presentation first. Then there was Herod's extermination of two-year-olds. Why that age? Presumably because that's how old Jesus was, suggesting a Magi visit two winters post-Nativity.

APOCRYPHA IN A PEAR TREE

While these are the stories and characters we find in the four Gospels, other Nativity stories abounded before the New Testament became canon in the early fourth century.

The second-century *Proto-Gospel of James* (Jesus' brother, who almost certainly didn't write it) includes a miraculous birth, but adds details: Joseph marrying a twelve-year-old Mary, chosen for her by priests in Nazareth, with a miraculous dove landing in the right place to select Joseph. When Mary becomes pregnant, a priest gives her and Joseph a potion that reveals lies, proving that her virginity is the truth. At Jesus' birth, time stands still – one of the earliest examples of the notion of time as a malleable, stoppable force, now taken for granted in science fiction.

Further unorthodox stories appear in the third-century *Questions of Bartholomew*, which includes an earthquake, and the *Epistles of the Apostles*, which equates Jesus with the Angel Gabriel, appearing to his own mother in advance of his birth.

The *Infancy Gospel of Pseudo-Matthew* was perhaps the apocryphal account that was most influential on how we think of Christmas today. It told how "the ox and the ass, having Him in their midst, incessantly adored Him". The ox and ass remained in Nativity scenes through the ages, despite never appearing in the four Gospels.

Then there were tales of animals talking at the moment of Jesus' birth. There were traditions of a shepherd girl following the shepherds in, but sobbing because she had no gift, and where she wept a miraculous Christmas rose suddenly grew. There were songs of Mary in an orchard, asking Joseph to pluck a cherry for her; Joseph refuses, so the cherry branch miraculously bows down for the fruit to fall into Mary's hand. One doesn't have to read too far between the lines to detect the subtext.

Centuries later, unusual cameos were still being added. In Catalonia, one bizarre character joined crib scenes by the eighteenth century: a defecating peasant. No one fully knows how or why "*El Caganer*" appeared, but no Catalan crib scene can be without him. Some suggest the filthy figurine is fertilizing the ground; others claim his squatting indicates the grotesqueness of the crucifixion – somehow.

FATHER CHRISTMAS, WHITE CHRISTMAS…

It's a shame that the shepherd girl didn't make it. One unfortunate quirk of the history books is that almost every named figure to shape our Western Christmas appears to be a white male; those by their side, or working under them, are barely recalled. White Christmas and Father Christmas stay the whole season.

How different would it have been if the shepherd girl had been given her moment? If the Crusades had returned with more culture than just spice for our mince pies, or if St Nicola was that woman bishop in Turkey? If Central or South America had given us more than just the poinsettia plant, or if a Charlotte Dickens were given the chance to write about Ebenezia Scrooge? Western history's patrilineal, Caucasian course has put buffers up on our story: instead it's the full English, American, and German, shaped by kings, ministers, and scholars. Let's not forget the Middle Eastern start to the story, and Mary's rather crucial role in it. Alas though, the shepherd girl didn't make the cut.

ORIGEN'S STORY

If these extrabiblical tales sound extraordinary, imagine the early church's scepticism. Before a confirmed and canonized New Testament, many were wary of the whole story. We know how origin stories work in today's popular culture. A popular hero's famous adventures typically concern his exploits as a young adult, and these tales gather a fan base. We can't get enough of him, so we long to know what came before. So new writing comes to the fore, exploring the backstory.

The early church took a long time to embrace this idea. In the decades between Jesus' crucifixion and the first gospel writings, the stories spread were of Jesus' adult life. The first writings, from Mark, don't mention the Nativity story; perhaps it was unknown to him. Luke wrote the Acts of the Apostles before his Gospel – so you could argue that it's a prequel.

Ultimately all four evangelists wrote at far greater length about Jesus' final week than his first years, though Christmas has been celebrated far more widely than Easter, perhaps because Easter is the more controversial. The world can agree that Jesus was born, and even celebrate it – without the leap of faith needed to celebrate the resurrection.

Some actively discouraged any celebration of Jesus' beginnings. The ironically named Origen, an early church father born in the late second century, thought that origin stories were sinful. The only biblical characters to celebrate their birthdays? Pharaoh and Herod, and both celebrated by putting someone to death – a hanged baker, a beheaded John the Baptist.

CHRISTMAS IS COMING...

...but not yet. Christmas wasn't celebrated in the lifetime of Jesus, with the New Testament dwelling on Jesus' teaching, his resurrection, and its after-effects, along with letters of encouragement from Paul and others to the growing Mediterranean church.

A century or so post-Nativity, there were Midnight Mass celebrations, but these were private, secret, solemn – and heretical. Sects were forming as Christianity found its footing. "Christ's Mass" was still a long way from being recognizable as Christmas, and certainly not publicly celebrated. Life for the early Christians was still dangerous in the Roman empire. In fact the Roman midwinter celebration might appear more familiar to us. The festive season was about to get rather bawdy.

LES FETES SATURNALES.
An de Rome 535.

J. D. Miger, Inv. et Del. *P. Baquoy, Sculp.*

**A Roman banquet to celebrate Saturnalia,
17–19 December, c. 100 BC**

Chapter 2

Roman Holiday

(753 BC–AD 325)

 *

We all love an office party. Alright, we tolerate an office party. Alright, we're forced to tolerate an office party so that we don't get sacked. Of all the customs of Christmas, this was one of the earliest to be invented, pre-dating even Christmas itself.

The Roman poet Juvenal observed that "two things only the people anxiously desire – bread and circuses". To this day, festive office parties still offer both, as staff from top brass to minimum wage are treated to food and entertainment – even if it is chicken in a basket and an office limbo championship.

So where else would the wacky, hierarchical Christmas party find its origins, but in the wacky, hierarchical Roman empire? Their winter celebrations were fixed in the calendar long before Juvenal, long before Christ. In this chapter we'll look at the Roman festival rather similar to Christmas, and see Christianity find its place on the world stage – before the heckling began.

THE TWELVE CENTURIES OF NON-CHRISTMAS

Roman civilization spanned 1,200 years, beginning as a kingdom in around 753 BC, becoming a powerful republic under various Julius Caesars (or as Latin scholars call them, the Julii Caesares – surely a band available for weddings), then a vast empire in 27 BC. Christianity popped up in the latter phase, but by then Rome had done enough conquering to know how to deal with new religions – and it wasn't all about feeding their fans to the lions. Where possible, they were incorporated, and not just into the digestive tracts of wild animals.

Roman culture developed across a millennium and over 4 million square kilometres, from Spain to Armenia. Such time and expanse meant maintaining a delicate balance between old and new was essential, as well-worn Roman myths and traditions were brought to the newly conquered. Romans adapted and innovated, and that included popularizing worship for their gods. They made worship fun, by turning it into a party.

The story of Christmas doesn't wait for the Roman empire to become Christian, which it does 300 years after Christ. While early church fathers like Origen were still deciding whether they wanted to celebrate his birth at all, the Romans just wanted to celebrate, including a festival that the poet Catullus called "the best of days".

IT'S BEGINNING TO LOOK A LOT LIKE SATURNALIA

Like other cultures, Roman festivals fell towards midwinter when the crops needed urging back to life. Not only that, winter was a time when people were, well, bored.

The Roman year was split in two: the "war season" of summer and the "home season" from October to March. Soldiers were more likely to be home in winter months, and farmers downed tools. The weather kept an otherwise outdoor society indoors, so it was a time for both dinner parties and political parties. Here in southern Europe, seasonal variations were less vital than in Norse winter wonderlands, but there were still harvests, so there was still a festival. The English would later think of a crazy title for such an occasion: "Harvest Festival".

The Romans saw a link between crop success and worship, especially of agricultural gods like Saturn. It was logical then for the Saturnalia festival to be built around the shortest day of the year, but what started as one day expanded as it gained popularity. It was two days by the time of Christ, a full week 100 years later, growing eventually to nearly a fortnight. Christmas creep started early.

Saturn was said to have ruled over a golden era of peace, when bumper crops meant no need to farm, or even for laws to govern people, since everything was in such abundance. Christmas through the ages has always harked back to supposedly greater times, and ancient Rome was no exception. The festivities were an attempt to recreate Saturn's glory days, all part of the Roman love of nostalgia. They were conservative people with a notion of *mos maiorum* – the passed-down "way of the elders". Werther's Originals for us, Saturnalia for them.

It's odd to think that in Jesus' thirty or so Decembers, this Saturnalia festival existed around him. So let's pinpoint AD 33's Saturnalia as our "second date of Christmas", purely because it's when Christianity begins its collision course with the Roman festival that affects the future of Christmas. When cultures collide, there are sparks, and traditions find new homes.

As in Christmases to come, the day would begin with all attending the place of worship, then a large banquet. Here the cries are not of "Merry Christmas!" but of the popular greeting of this festival: "*Io Saturnalia!*"

On our second date of Christmas…
(Rome, 17 December AD 33)

Religious rite always comes first. Gather at the temple, where the statue of Saturn normally has his feet tied by woollen bands. The first act is to free these bands, liberating Saturn to join the party.

There's a sacrifice, then a meal, primarily for Saturn himself, whose graven image reclines on a couch reserved for the guest of honour. He is part of the banquet, the convivium publicum, *where all dine – but only after Saturn gets the good stuff.*

The celebrations move homeward where the festival continues. Work is banned at all levels: there can be no declaration of war or court business. Instead it's a time for drinking, dancing, and debauchery, the wealthy enjoying wine, the poor on the beer.

Thankfully slavery doesn't count as work, though even they get some of the day off. That's not so much about being nice at not-called-Christmas, as it is about something at the very heart of the festival: the topsy-turvy factor.

Slaves are served dinner by their masters (although the slaves cooked it); they might swap clothes and play games together. Overdue bills might even be written off, and on even rarer occasions, slaves might be freed. It's unlikely given another custom – this is when masters dwell on the end-of-year finance report, and ask gods for help with the year ahead. (Even office parties often come with a board meeting.)

The next two days are public holidays. On the latter, 19 December, gifts known as sigillariae are given. Like workplace presents, these aren't extravagant displays of one-upmanship, but token novelty gifts like candles or pottery. Wax figurines are popular too, a nod to earlier days of actual human sacrifice (the wax versions are a lot less messy). Little verses might accompany the pressies, a precursor to the greeting cards, that are delayed 2,000 years in the post.

Some gifts are hung in earthenware boxes, inspiring another future tradition where empty boxes are filled by employers to thank their tradesmen. By the twenty-first century the boxes may be lost, but Boxing Day will remain.

A "King of Saturnalia" is chosen by lot: a raucous Master of Ceremonies, assuming the role of Saturn himself and giving out dares. In old days it was a poisoned role; the chosen Master of Ceremonies was put to death to end the festival – clown as sacrifice. He wears a mock crown, showing that he, the Commander-in-Cheekiness, is issuing the orders: "Cover him with cold water! Sing naked! Do the Macarena! Alright, do the Latin equivalent of it! I don't know, the Macaren-us…" His flimsy crown is deliberately not built to last. Centuries later, cracker-pulling partygoers will find the crown's durability hasn't improved much.

The enforced fun has its boundaries, and the slaves are wise not to overstep the mark. They have what the poet Horace calls "December liberty", but talk too frankly with the boss, and there may be consequences when normal service resumes. Then again, Roman society is more home-based than others, meaning that slaves overhear a lot. Gossip abounds – so the master–slave relationship is best kept happy. The empire is built on slavery – this annual humbling of pomposity and general shindig for slaves ensures that the imperial wheels keep turning.

SATURNALIA'S ALRIGHT FOR FIGHTING

Like the modern Christmas, Saturnalia could get out of hand. The writer Pliny was a bit of a Scroogius Maximus, taking himself to secluded rooms "…when the rest of the house is noisy with the licence of the holiday and festive cries. This way I don't hamper the games of my people, and they don't hinder my work or studies."

For the most part the atmosphere was of communal joy, partly thanks to Greek influence – civility, flair – on this Roman institution. This air of bonhomie made it attractive to all comers – even early Christians, unknowingly eyeing it up for their own festive takeover.

For some time after Christ, there was still no Christianity. It was not a religion; there were no Scriptures. Pockets of followers, who had either witnessed Jesus first-hand or heard of him, were cropping up across the empire, thanks to Mediterranean trade routes and the scattering of the disciples. The seeds of Christianity were planted on the shores of southern Europe, but growth takes time. These new Christians were living in Roman, Greek, and Jewish culture; they absorbed customs without even knowing it – even if they didn't join in.

Three office party traditions we didn't QUITE get from the Romans...

✧ *"DISCUS JOCKIUS"...* Saturnalia's mock king reoccurs throughout Christmas history – the medieval "Lord of Misrule", the French "Abbot of Unreason", the Catholic "Boy Bishop", and our modern party host. The Roman version mostly bossed people about "hilariously". It's doubtful he took requests for the bangingest minstrel tunes: "A maximus shout-out to Julie from Accounts. She wants us to do a new dance called The Conga, so come on everybody..."

✧ *"RUMPUS-POMPEY IN CUPBOARDUS STATIONERIA"...* The Romans weren't averse to parties of sex, drugs, and lute 'n' roll. If the master of the house overstepped the mark with a slave-girl (or slave-boy for that matter), he probably wouldn't see the need for a cupboard.

✧ *VISITING THE SHRINE OF "PHOTOCOPIA"...* If they had them, I'm certain they'd be lifting their togas and sitting on one before you can say: "No, slave, you can't have a pay rise."

KALENDS

Days after Saturnalia, it was time for another festival, just as New Year follows Christmas. Kalends lasted from the 1st to the 3rd of January and featured yet more days off work – after all, the farmers and soldiers had downed tools and swords. There was more feasting and more gifts, called *strenae*: lucky greenery, cakes, or just cold hard cash. Missing an opportunity, they didn't just pass on unwanted Saturnalia gifts – I know I would.

Only in the last 100 or so years have we stopped giving New Year gifts as they did. If it seems like the Romans were doing a lot of gift-giving, yes they were – but then with such a vast empire, they were a materialistic bunch. Why not demonstrate your affection, or wealth, by showing off some exotic item imported from across the Mediterranean? Better than a book token.

Kalends Eve (their New Year's Eve) was marked with singing, "leaping", dressing up in animal skins, and general all-night mischief. At daybreak, the partygoers returned home and (presumably drunkenly) attempted to decorate their homes. It sounds hilarious, and really we should all emulate this one Christmas and see how it looks.

The first day of Kalends was the first day of the year, and after sleeping off the late night, folks might gather to receive money distributed by the authorities. The second day featured more dice gambling between master and slave, and the third day might feature chariot racing. On the fourth day, those decorations might start to come down. If you're thinking this sounds like an awesome festival, you're about right – all that's missing is a massive feast.

I forgot to mention – they would also have a massive feast. This is all very civilized, but that's domestic life under the Romans for you. The very notion of "a home", to thrive in rather than just to live in, was still new, so home décor, furniture, and lifestyle were fashionable concepts. Other Europeans may have celebrated outside, but now holly, fir, and laurel were commonly brought inside, perhaps placed over the fireplace to protect from evil spirits entering down the chimney. (A legendary creature entering the home down the chimney at Christmas? That may catch on.)

Kalends gives us the word "calendar", and it gave the Romans yet another festival for their calendar. And between Saturnalia and Kalends, they had room for one more…

DRIVING HOME FOR MITHRAS

Roman religious life was certainly cluttered – a bit like the next whistle-stop tour, so bear with us. The more cultures conquered, the more gods and temples jostled for attention – and that meant even more feast days. By the mid-first century, 159 days of the year were festival days, and more than half veered towards the raucous. Romans worked hard but played hard too. It's not just in recent years that religious midwinter festivals have been a time for kicking back or partying hard, rather than simply worship of the divine.

Vying with Christianity for attention was Mithraism: for a time the most popular religion in the Roman world. While Christianity was still gathering its Scriptures and forming its church, fans flocked to Mithras. Mithras was worshipped, and called the "sun of righteousness", drawing on a reference in the Old Testament book of Malachi. (Wait a while, and "Hark! The Herald Angels…" sings of Christ as the "Son of Righteousness".) Other than this, its origins weren't Judaic, but Persian or Zoroastrian. This religion was not a development of Judeo-Christianity, but a rival.

Mithraism benefitted from a couple of boosts. Firstly soldiers liked it, so they helped it travel, and looked forward to journeying home to celebrate each December. Secondly, ah yes – December. Mithras inherited a birthday when his religion linked with *sol invictus*, a Roman sun god cult made official by Emperor Aurelian in AD 274. This meant inheriting the Festival of the Birthday of the Unconquered Sun (*dies natalis solis invicti* – about as catchy in both languages) on the winter solstice, which in the Julian calendar was 25 December.

It was a popular festival of lights in this darkest time of the year, which once again meant candles and fire. If Christianity was eyeing up anyone's date (always awkward in any social environment), it would be that of a liberating "god of sun", to be replaced by the liberating "Son of God".

Writing in 1882's *The History of the Origins of Christianity*, Ernest Renan suggested "if Christianity had been impeded in its growth by some mortal malady, the world would be Mithraic". Instead Mithraism suffered that malady (thankfully – I can't even say "Merry Mithrmas"), largely because it had no scriptures, women were denied entry, and the levels of initiation were complex. But emperors up to Constantine identified with the religion, even including representations of Mithras on coinage.

THE BATTLE FOR CHRISTIANITY

Mithraism started later and blossomed sooner, but Christianity's popularity was growing steadily. Its trump card was open access to all, with particular attention to the poor and the sick. Word spread of Jesus' Beatitudes from The Sermon on the Mount: "Blessed are the meek… the poor in spirit… the peacemakers…" It was an attractive religion for the Roman underclass – everyone could join a faith of love, liberation, and hope, no matter your ethnicity, gender, or wealth.

This appeal meant that while Jewish converts might be whole families shifting faith, gentiles often made the leap on their own. Roman households might feature a slave or family member who'd attend these new house churches. Roman religion was an outdoor event, but Christian churches were necessarily indoors, undercover, with a shared communion bonding its followers.

This meant a slow and steady growth, which was scary to Rome. So top-down Christian punishment and scapegoating were harsh – too harsh for many civilized Roman citizens. They knew converts, lived with them, or employed them. Mithras might have been on the coins and Christianity the underdog, but "Render unto Caesar the things that are Caesar's" – and "First shall be last and last shall be first".

Seven emperors and Christianity – a hate-hate-hate-hate-like-love-love relationship...

✧ *NERO (54–68 AD)...* Just under a quarter of post-Christian emperors picked on Christians. Nero especially blamed them for Rome's fire, to take attention away from his own rumoured involvement. His punishments were severe – see *Game of Thrones* (I don't mean he made them watch *Game of Thrones*) – and included the martyrdoms of Peter and Paul.

✧ *DOMITIAN (81–96 AD)...* riled Christians by calling himself "Lord and God". Riled them even more by killing them.

✧ *DECIUS (249–251)...* ordered the first empire-wide persecution of Christians, requiring official certificates that they'd offered pagan sacrifices – or death certificates.

- *DIOCLETIAN (284–305)…* ordered The Great Persecution of Christians in 303. Christian homes and books were destroyed; prisoners were massacred simply due to too many arrests. The only benefit? It sparked intrigue from Romans about their unrecantable beliefs.

- *GALERIUS (305–311)…* The Edict of Galerius ended the persecution, but property wasn't returned – and not just because it was rubble.

- *CONSTANTINE (306–337)…* grew up in the sun god cult, but his mum was a Christian ex-stable-maid. He converted at the Battle of Milvian Bridge, glancing at the sun to see a cross with a Greek slogan: "In this sign, conquer!" He daubed a cross on his troops' shields, and though outnumbered five to one, they won. His Edict of Milan in 313 granted tolerance to all religions, returning Christian property and encouraging church-building.

- *JUSTINIAN (527–565)…* made Christmas an official civic holiday throughout the empire – or what was left of it. By now it was the Byzantine empire – sort of Roman-lite, like the old turf but without the fatty western bits.

PAGAN GONE

By 336, Christmas was being celebrated in Rome in some form. In 350, Pope Julius I declared that 25 December was Christ's official birthday, and within four years there were public Christian celebrations on that date. In 380, Christianity became the official state religion, and pagan cults were outlawed. Do they know it's Mithras? Not any more they don't. *Dies natalis* dies, and the Unconquered Sun is conquered. Saturnalia – what-urnalia? Kalends ends – but not just yet.

Kalends clung on, as a secular festival; the only prostration here was from too much booze. Christians frowned upon it, encouraging believers to fast not feast. But these festivals were popular; Christianity may have been expanding, but it had a PR battle on its hands.

X MARKS THE SPOT

As Christmas spread west and east, it grew in both Roman and Greek cultures. On the Roman side, the serious Norse Yule had been filtered through the jollier Saturnalia (because it's all about "bread and circuses") before finally giving the world its Christmas.

On the Greek side, there was colourful decorative culture, and even an ancestor of the carol as children toured with songs and olive branches. It's the Greeks we thank for abbreviating Christmas to "Xmas", since their "X" – "*chi*" – is the first letter and symbol for Christ. So any present-day abbreviators – you're not being lazy, you're being classically Greek. You can tell that to your Xian friends, or anyone called Xopher, or singers Xina Aguilera or Tony Xie.

TWO FOUNDING FATHER-(CHRISTMAS)S

Christianity's state-sanctioned boom led to localized differences and big questions. As we all know, if you want a good, clear outcome, form a council. You won't get that outcome, but you can watch a lot of people brawl to take your mind off things. Gladiatorial games stopped just a few years after these councils met. Coincidence? (Yes.)

The Council of Nicaea in 325 serves as a handy historical bridge. It had nothing to do with Christmas, but two of its attendees massively impacted on how we celebrate.

The first was Emperor Constantine, who secured the future of Christianity. He convened this council to address issues of Jesus' divinity, create a new creed, and rule on how we date Easter (it's the fourth Sunday after the one before the ninth week if the year's got a four in it… oh forget it, this book's on Christmas).

Surely no other attendee could warrant an even bigger presence in our story? Yet one of the invited bishops, from the Eastern church, went on to become the very face of Christmas. He never knew it in his lifetime – nor in fact did he see either the date of Christmas or the New Testament canon confirmed. Imprisoned under Diocletian, freed under Constantine – meet St Nicholas.

St Nicholas ascends to heaven, Bishop of Myra,
St Nicolas de Veroce church

Chapter 3

Ho Ho Who?

(270–1100)

Our round-the-world sleigh ride has already stopped in Scandinavia, Palestine, and the Roman empire. Now we guide it in to land in Asia Minor, our modern-day Turkey. The man we'll visit would probably have never seen a sleigh, or a reindeer. The only visual aspect in common with our Santa Claus is Nicholas of Myra's long white beard.

Before the beard, before the legend, before the bishop, was the boy. Nikolaos, to give his Greek name, was born in around 270 to wealthy Greek parents in the busy Mediterranean port town of Patara, living along the coast in Myra in Lycia. Yes, Nicholas began life, like Christmas stuffing, in Turkey.

He was named after his uncle, Bishop Nicholas of Patara, and the whole family were part of a small Christian community possibly founded by St Paul himself 200 years earlier. The legends surrounding Nicholas began early – one story tells that as a newborn, he stood up on the altar for several hours, raising hands heavenwards as if in prayer. Another legend holds that even as a baby, he abstained from breastfeeding for the traditional two fasting days each week (the original 5:2 plan). When he did feed, it was only ever from the right breast, so loyal to God's right hand was the infant Nicholas.

More historically reported is the early demise of his parents after an epidemic, so the boy moved in with his uncle the bishop, and trained under him as a priest. After the Great Persecution, Nicholas made a pilgrimage to Bethlehem and spent several years on retreat in nearby caves. On returning home, he became Bishop of Myra. It isn't known at which point he grew the beard – we can assume it was after he was a boy, but with Nicholas, it seems anything was possible.

In this chapter we'll look at Nicholas' life and legend, hear some bells, and meet some truly horrific Christmas creatures.

NICAEA TO SEE YOU, TO SEE YOU...

That Council of Nicaea was crucial in the establishment of the early Christian church. Emperor Constantine invited 1,800 bishops, including Nicholas, in the hope of emerging with clear answers on the divinity of Jesus, rather than the various theories put forward by different Christian thinkers. There were the early church fathers, and then there were those who were a little off-kilter. Let's maybe call them early church uncles, or early church babysitters-with-slightly-unorthodox-parenting-methods-so-when-you-pick-the-child-up-it's-a-bit-different.

To encourage attendance, travel and lodging were free, yet only 300 bishops attended. There was also a man called Arius who, though not a bishop, was the champion of Arianism – well, it was named after him. He believed that Jesus was created by God, coming after God the Father, and therefore subordinate to Him. Nicholas was so vehemently anti-Arian that it's said he punched Arius in the face. One legend has it that his peers were so shocked they instantly called for his dismissal as bishop – till Jesus and Mary appeared as visions alongside him, and the bishops for some reason thought better of it and awkwardly consulted their minutes.

This uncharacteristic display of aggression belies a passionate defender of the faith, whose chief temperament was simple generosity. Ever since inheriting the family wealth, Nicholas had quietly been dispensing with it. With no family that we know of, Nicholas had little use for the money, instead opting to give much away to those in need. One particular story threw him into the history books faster than you can throw a bag of gold through a window into a stocking.

STOCKING-FILLERS

Word reached Nicholas of a local widower with three daughters, poor business sense, and very little money. Nicholas' fortunate circumstances were down to his parents' good investments, so he was inclined to help the man. The fellow needed a dowry to pay for each daughter to be married and their futures secured. Failing that, slavery or prostitution were the only options left.

Nicholas waited till dark and placed a bag of gold through a downstairs window of the house – it was for the eldest daughter, and according to legend it landed in one of her socks hanging by the fireplace, or perhaps in one of the shoes warming by the fireside. Some time later, Nicholas repeated the undercover charitable act for the second daughter.

By now the father was puzzled. He had one daughter left and one more chance to catch the anonymous donor, so he stayed up night after night by the window. He eventually saw Nicholas in the act – the only person ever to catch Santa Claus red-handed. (By the twentieth century, pretty much the only part of St Nicholas not to be red would be his white-gloved hands. Ah, irony.)

The bishop swore the father to secrecy over his identity as the mystery benefactor, not wanting the world to latch onto his free payouts. Nicholas chose his recipients carefully based on need rather than a queue outside his house. But the father couldn't restrain his gratitude and spread word of Nicholas' generosity – and presumably his mean aim at basketball.

MORE THAN A BISHOP

Nicholas was respected as a fair and equitable leader and representative of the region. On one occasion he was begged by his townspeople to ask Emperor Constantine for much-needed tax relief. Nicholas made the long journey and succeeded in the negotiation, immediately attaching the emperor's written order to a stick before throwing it into the sea. The order then somehow made its way across the Mediterranean, was discovered, and was taken to the local authorities in Myra. An unorthodox postal system, but like they say, post early for Christmas.

Before Nicholas left for home, Constantine summoned him back and rescinded the order for lower tax, following a brisk meeting with his Finance Minister. But it was too late. Nicholas told the emperor that the order had already been put into effect back home, thanks to his ingenious (and alright, not historically verified) method of sea-mail. When Constantine sent a runner to check, he was aghast and impressed, so let the lower rate of taxation stand.

Perhaps the real miracle is how a story about taxation lasted the centuries, but if anyone can do it, Nicholas can…

On our third date of Christmas…
(Turkey, 6 December 343)

At the ripe age of seventy-three, that perpetual donor Nicholas of Myra gives his last. By now he is a local celebrity, well-reputed for putting coins into the shoes townsfolk leave outside their homes, on the off chance he's passing. Now this not-so-secret benefactor has passed from life into legend, his good deeds may stop but the tales will continue.

The tales quickly grow tall, and as a great traveller, Nicholas has given us plenty to choose from. One story sees him stopping at an inn to discover that the innkeeper has been slaughtering boys and pickling them in brine, to sell on as ham. Nicholas not only saves three boys but actually reassembles them after the innkeeper's butchering.

Then there's the tale of how he helped locals in a famine. The crops were failing, so when a ship carrying wheat docked at port, Bishop Nicholas asked for a donation. The sailors' cargo had been purchased for the emperor, so they refused. Nicholas persuaded them that if they gave some of their wheat to the hungry locals, by the time their ship unloaded in Alexandria, the weight would miraculously be restored. They agreed, and sure enough, not only were the people of Myra kept in wheat for years, but when the ship was unloaded all of the grain was somehow still there. Anecdotes like this paint the bishop as not only generous and godly but also fair to all, and not just giving but enabling others to give too.

The miraculous tales ensure Nicholas' sainthood. One has him being rewarded in Jerusalem by the church doors of the Room of the Last Supper; they swung open to greet him as he approached, in possibly the world's first recorded automatic door.

Nicholas' tomb becomes a shrine. Sailors in particular often pay tribute, in thanks for Nicholas' many journeys and miracles with them. As they travel, they take stories with them, legends as cargo, which all helps St Nicholas become the most popular saint in the world.

RIGHT PLACE, RIGHT TIME (RIGHT FANS)

Nicholas' shrine gained great footfall thanks to its coastal position, and nearby Constantinople becoming the centre of Christendom. Constantine's new-build city was taking over from Rome as the seat of the emperor – much nearer the new battle-lines. Unusually, he insisted on Christian churches being built, but no other temples, since official pagan sacrifices had just been stopped by the state. Christianity was no longer an underground movement, so saints like St Nick were now in vogue.

The empire couldn't quite decide though which flavour of

Christianity to support. There weren't as many as there used to be thanks to unifying councils like Nicaea, and it took a few more centuries for the church to fully split into Eastern (Orthodox) and Western (Catholic). But the Eastern side was growing that bit faster in the years after Nicholas' death, thanks to accidental missionaries like sailors and soldiers spreading the news. The Eastern church's growth meant that Nicholas' tomb was fast becoming a top Mediterranean tourist attraction.

By the 900s, that prolific Greek writer Anonymous (or they might have been anonymous) told how "the West as well as the East acclaims and glorifies him. Wherever there are people, his name is revered and churches are built in his honour." Pilgrims particularly visited on the anniversary of Nicholas' death. Nearly 2,000 years on, St Nicholas' Day is still celebrated across the planet. In many countries, 6 December rather than the 25th is the day to give gifts, in tribute to the humble generosity, that open window, those stockings, and the crack-shot aim of St Nick.

IT'S IN THE BOOK

St Nicholas had nothing to do with Christmas for centuries – for many across Europe, he still doesn't, with his saint's day celebrations being kept entirely separate from Christmas. While Nicholas' legend was slowly spreading, one of his peers, Bishop Athanasius of Alexandria (also at the Council of Nicaea, though as a deacon at the time), wrote a letter in the year 367, documenting the twenty-seven accepted books of the New Testament.

The four Gospels had become canon. The Nativity accounts of Matthew and Luke were enshrined in history, while apocryphal accounts such as the *Proto-Gospel of James* were set aside. The outcome was the Nativity story we now recognize: shepherds, wise men… and no talking animals.

There's evidence too that in around 380, a Christian Roman family had a picture of Jesus, Mary, and Joseph hung in their tomb. Perhaps this was the first proper Christmas decoration. Alright it was year-round rather than just seasonal, but the family were a little restricted when it came to taking it down.

THE FIRST TWELVE DAYS OF CHRISTMAS

By the early fifth century, Rome was celebrating Midnight Mass on Christmas Eve. But while Christmas celebrations were burgeoning in the West, Eastern folks were more reluctant, even though their brand of Christianity was spreading faster. Not for the last time, we see that Christianity and Christmas were taking slightly different paths.

East and West even celebrated on different dates. The twenty-fifth of December had been the Western Christmas for 200 years, but Eastern churches preferred 6 January, the day of both Jesus' baptism and the visit of the Magi. Perhaps celebrating the baptism not the birthday puts greater significance on spiritual birth over earthly birth. To this day, 6 January is Orthodox Christmas Eve.

In 567, France hosted the Council of Tours (the original "Tours de France") to settle several key disputes of the day. These included the marital state of clergy (monks should live in dormitories not cells; women shouldn't be allowed in monasteries – and you know I'm talking to you, Sister Florence…) and when exactly to celebrate Christmas.

To satisfy both sides of the church, the twelve days between the Western church's 25 December and the Eastern church's 6 January were in their entirety deemed holy days – or "holidays". After all, if the Romans could extend Saturnalia from one day to nearly a fortnight, why couldn't Christmas grow a little too? Christmas has always been a time for an expanding waistline, and timeline.

So the origin of our twelve days of Christmas – telling us when to take down our decorations, or a ditty about five gold rings and a partridge – is built on compromise, to satisfy both sides of the church. Because what are Christmas holidays about, if not keeping both sides of the family happy?

THAT RINGS A BELL...

From the early fifth century, Christmas found a new soundtrack. St Paulinus was a poet, a senator, and Governor of Campania in Italy before giving up politics for religion, becoming Bishop of Nola. "Campania" means "countryside" in Latin and gives us "campanology" – bell-ringing. The first campanile, or bell-tower, was built on Paulinus' watch (not his wrist-watch, though we can probably thank him for your watch alarm too).

In his area of Italy, they produced the bronze that made sturdy bells, and it's said that Paulinus thought to put these in even sturdier belfries. They'd be rung to call people to worship, spread news of births, marriages, and deaths, and tell the locals when it was a festival day like Easter (said to be a three-bell occasion) or Christmas (a four-beller).

Far beyond the church, in darker lands, bells were already used to scare off evil spirits in the dead of winter. If you haven't got a flame, you can make a noise, and bells were a cheap, easy way of doing that. Sleigh bells long pre-date Santa, St Nick, and Christmas; the earliest horses and camels were draped in bells, like an ancient car horn (to warn folks you're coming) or car alarm (to stop them stealing your ride). Further north, on reindeer, they were extra useful in the dark, fog, or snow – even Santa needs help finding where he parked his vehicle.

That quote from *It's a Wonderful Life* – "Every time a bell rings, an angel gets its wings..." – came long before the movie. For a century before, children associated Christmas with bells. Sleigh bells went into production in the United States in Connecticut in 1810, while handbells became fashionable in Victorian England. Christmas bells thus have no set size, from oversized church bell to sleigh bell to hand-held instrument. Before carols there was campanology: the bell was the Christmas number one.

POSTHUMOUS TALES

As Christmas found its place in church and its calendar, St Nicholas was still finding his place – and that included where his bones were kept.

New stories appeared with new generations of sailors – some even set long after the saint's death, as new miracles were attributed to him. Sailors would pray for Nicholas to intervene and save them from shipwrecks – the ones who made it back would say they survived because of St Nicholas (the ones who didn't make it back, well, wouldn't have a chance to say otherwise).

Some posthumous stories reinforced the notion of his protection of children. In one, the townsfolk of Myra were celebrating on his saint day when some Cretan pirates looted the church and stole a local boy while they were there. Returning to Crete, the boy, named Basilios, was presented to their king or "emir", serving him as a cup-bearing slave for a full year. At the next St Nicholas' Day a year later, Basilios' family held a quiet remembrance at home while the town's celebrations continued as usual. They prayed for the boy's safe keeping, on which St Nicholas intervened and whisked him away from the emir's side. A confused Basilios instantly appeared to his parents, still holding the cup he was about to give the Cretan king.

A MOVING STORY

With miraculous stories like this (and an easily lootable seaside town), Nicholas' relics were fiercely guarded. Alright, that may be overstating it. There were four Orthodox monks, but that's still more than guard most graves.

But wars and conquests saw the area change: the Turks defeated the Byzantines, and the occupying forces went back and forth. Famous relics like those of St Nicholas should surely be housed elsewhere… it was selflessly suggested by places that wanted to host them. They did have a point though: a pilgrimage site further west might secure the future for what was left of the good saint.

The Italian coastal cities of Venice and Bari both vied to rehome the bones, as modern-day cities pitch to host the Olympics. Bari sailors got a jump on the Venetians, by nipping past the four monks and hightailing it with St Nicholas, like a medieval *Ocean's Eleven* (emphasis on "Ocean"). The relics arrived in their new shrine on 9 May 1087, helping Bari to become a popular stopping-point for crusaders to and from the Holy Land.

Venice won too, by the way. The Bari sailors only managed to smuggle out half of the skeleton, so smaller fragments remained in Nicholas' original grave, till some passing Venetian sailors swung by a decade later and nabbed those too. They've only recently been tested: the bones in Bari's Basilica di San Nicola *and* in Venice's San Nicolò al Lido both belong to the same skeleton. Both cities still attract thousands of tourists each year to visit their respective parts of St Nick. (They're missing a trick by not offering a discount if you visit the full set.)

MYRA, MYRRH IS ON THE WALL...

Before we're stolen away from Myra like Nicholas' bones, there is one last Christmas link to the place. Myra was so-named after the substance that grew in its mountains: myrrh. Not only was this familiar as one of the Magi's gifts, but the liquid was said to emanate from St Nicholas' bones. Those who visited would seek it out and apply it like a healing balm, and it's still produced today from his new tomb in Bari. (You could argue that St Nick still brings people soothing balms to be rubbed into their skin each December, though it's no miracle – you can buy it in the chemist.)

Twenty-eight patronages of St Nicholas...

✧ *SAILORS*... because of miraculous stories of Nicholas helping sailors.

✧ *CHILDREN*... because of miraculous stories of Nicholas helping children.

✧ *STUDENTS*... because children then become students.

✧ *MAIDENS OR VIRGINS*... because Nicholas threw money through a window to help three maidens.

✧ *PROSTITUTES*... because the maidens nearly became prostitutes.

✧ *PAWNBROKERS*... because he gave money when needed – to this day, almost every sign on a pawnbrokers' shop contains three gold balls, representing the three sacks of gold Nicholas threw through the window.

✧ *PERFUMERIES*... because of the myrrh.

✧ *MERCHANTS, PIRATES, JUDGES, PRISONERS, PENITENT THIEVES, PHARMACISTS, BARREL-MAKERS, ARCHERS, COOPERS, THE POOR, SHOE-SHINERS, PILGRIMS, BRIDES, GROOMS, NEWLY-WEDS AND SPINSTERS, ABERDEEN, LIVERPOOL,*

GREECE (ESPECIALLY THE NAVY), RUSSIA… it goes on. A Russian expression goes as follows: "If God dies, at least we'll still have St Nicholas."

LEGEND BECOMES MYTH

St Nicholas was literally becoming an icon and a cult figure. He had moved from life to legend, and now legend to myth. His bones were moved to Italy but the stories were taken further, as Dutch ships brought news of him to Northern Europe. In this land of Norse gods and ancient winter rites, the cult of St Nicholas took hold on a whole new level.

The Roman empire's ban of paganism hadn't reached here, so St Nicholas was a good fit with Norse worship of other bearded folk like Odin and Thor. Merging with Odin over time, Nicholas was pictured with full beard and bishop's robe, flying through the sky on a horse as Odin did. Thanks to this Northern European iconography, St Nick transformed from kind earthly traveller to a robed figure riding an animal through the sky, though for the time being his horse let no reindeer join in the games.

ELF-EMPLOYED

Odin the All-father was a Norse version of a pre-Christian deity called Wotan, worshipped by some old Teutonic tribes in ancient Europe. Wotan was said to ride through the sky on a Wild Hunt, collecting dead souls as he flew through the air. Happy Christmas, everybody…

The Finns merged the wagon's driver with the goat bucks leading the way, to make *Joulupukki* ("Yule buck"), a goat-man said to wear tight red leather trousers and coat. Eventually he merged further with his more familiar American counterpart, so today he's almost indistinguishable from Santa Claus. *Joulupukki* is no chimney-botherer though; he knocks on the door asking, "Are there well-behaved children here?" Only in Finnish.

As for Odin, he had more than just sleigh-driving skill – he employed a host of elves and spirits. He had a horse, an eight-legged beast called Sleipnir, who would help him place gifts in shoes that children had left out for him, in folklore seemingly borrowed back from St Nicholas. These elements changed hands and became attached to the St Nicholas myth. Those crazy stories of levelling out the grain weight seem quite normal now, don't they?

ADDING TO THE CHRISTMAS STEW

The interchange of ideas between religions is complex and varied, and Christianity too was inheriting back parts of the new version of the saint they'd originally donated north. Catholic and Eastern Orthodox veneration of St Nicholas became interlaced with ideas of this tall robed giant of a man, wrapped up warm for a Northern winter, rather than the inconspicuous Mediterranean bishop who travelled in disguise and was probably about five feet tall.

Other cultures threw in further elements. In Lapland, a tribal shaman would lead festivities by consuming hallucinogenic mushrooms to feel as if he were flying through the sky, to convey the message of the totemic "Reindeer Spirit".

Why reindeer? Well, eating the mushrooms direct doesn't go down too well, so instead they'd use reindeer as a filter, feeding them the magic mushrooms first, collecting their urine in a bucket, and voila: a delicacy to be passed around like the wassail bowls we'll hear about shortly. Only this one doesn't just make you drunk – it makes you fly like Odin, or St Nick, or the reindeer. I think they're taking the pee – or at least the tee-pee, because like a teepee, each yurt would be entered via the smokehole in the roof. Centuries before Santa popped down our chimneys before flying off with his reindeer, shamans would pop down chimneys with a reindeer-wee-based flight simulator.

DUTCH COURAGE

The Netherlands, whose sailors imported St Nicholas to northern climes in the first place, have always had a particular fondness for their Sinterklaas. Like Odin, Sinterklaas has a horse, though the Dutch version is a white horse called Amerigo who rides across rooftops, while Odin's is grey and flies higher. Odin was said to give letters (or "runes") from on high; Sinterklaas gives chocolate letters to children.

Ably assisting Sinterklaas is Zwarte Piet – Black Peter. This character has fallen out of favour over the last few years, especially in terms of dressing up in blackface to represent him, but he has staunch Dutch defenders who insist it's nothing to do with race – it's tradition. Historically they're right – Piet's colour was from Odin's black ravens who'd report to him on what mankind was up to; similarly Zwarte Piet would report to Sinterklaas on the behaviour of children. Whether or not elements of the slave trade helped the tradition prosper, I'm not qualified to say – all I know is that Piet is still fondly thought of in the Netherlands today. In 2013, 92 per cent of the Dutch public thought the Zwarte Piet character was nothing to do with race or slavery.

Sinterklaas arrives from Spain by boat each 6 December, and Dutch ports still host this impressive spectacle. The boat represents St Nick's role as patron to sailors, while Spain may represent his bones lying in Bari (which was sometimes Italian, sometimes Spanish, depending on who was winning what war).

Another theory is based on St Nicholas' iconography always including three gold balls, the sacks that he threw into that window many years before. By the time these images reached the

Netherlands, the story had been confused. The best guess was that the picture was of three oranges. And where do the Dutch get their oranges from? Spain.

It's a convincing story. French nuns started the habit (actually better not call it a habit) of leaving socks full of tangerines and nuts outside the houses of the needy – which at last explains why I found a satsuma in my stocking every Christmas. My parents certainly never knew how it got there. Must have been a passing nun.

Six ho ho horror stories...

✧   *KNECHT RUPRECHT...* Germany in particular saw St Nicholas pick up unlikely companions, including this rather frightening elf, a manservant rescued and fostered by St Nicholas from a young age. Knecht Ruprecht would ask children if they could pray; those who could were rewarded with fruit and gingerbread, but those who couldn't were given lumps of coal, or a beating, or a beating with a bag full of lumps of coal. Knecht Ruprecht was Santa's little helper – and still is on a certain animated TV show. In the German version of *The Simpsons*, the family dog isn't known as Santa's Little Helper; he's Knecht Ruprecht.

✧   *BELSNICKEL AND KRAMPUS...* Not a cheery double act. The masked, long-tongued Belsnickel carries a switch for beating, and has a horned goat-like chum, the Krampus. They could be kind, but their punishing nature is now the stuff of horror films. Oh, they're also of Germanic origin. You probably knew that.

✧   *JULNISSEN...* Scandinavian cheeky elves, who live in attics and mischievously hide gifts around the house (perhaps helped out by the odd parent).

✧ *CALLICANTZARI…* Drifting into the downright nasty, the Greeks have horrible little creatures who live underground and spend all year gnawing away at the roots of the Tree of Life to try to bring all life crashing down for good. The jawbones of pigs would be hung to ward off these little monstrosities, and fires would burn all season to keep them at bay.

✧ *THE CHRISTMAS LADS…* Not a work party gone out of hand – these are thirteen Icelandic trolls, who roam houses for thirteen days before Christmas. Each of their names is a Dahlesque BFG-like wonder: Bowl-Licker hides under beds waiting for someone to put their dinner on the floor, Sausage-Swiper snatches bangers while they're being cooked, and you might hear Door-Slammer or catch sight of Window-Peeper. But their chief aim? To steal children… but only the naughty ones, so you'd better be good for goodness' sake.

✧ *ST NICHOLAS…* Lest we forget that St Nick himself wasn't always painted as a generous gold-thrower. William Caxton's 1483 book of saints, *Legenda Aurea*, noted that he could be "cruel in correctyng", whipping naughty children. Jolliness will follow.

MARTINMAS

Back in church, Catholic adoration of St Nicholas continued, even surviving the Reformation amid Protestant attempts to see off the saints. But there were of course countless other saints celebrated year-round.

St Martin was another favourite, his saint's day being just ahead of the Christmas season on 11 November. When alive, he was Bishop Martin of Tours, a contemporary of St Nicholas. He too was a generous man, known for cutting his cloak in half to warm a freezing beggar. His list of patronages was nearly as long as that of St Nicholas, including being the patron saint of hoteliers, soldiers, and the perhaps opposing areas of both vintners and reformed alcoholics.

Martinmas was popular throughout Europe for centuries, with bonfires lit on Martinmas Eve. As the weather turned cold, animals that couldn't be fed through winter might be sacrificed – if they'd die anyway, they might as well as be put to use. In the late first millennium, Advent began the very next day with a fierce forty-day fast – so Martinmas was the last chance to stuff those cheeks, and the first of the new wine was drunk in celebration. German children would place cups of water outside of their doors, plus a horseshoe-shaped biscuit for his trusty steed. If St Martin were to ride by, the water might change to wine (although perhaps Dad had better help you drink that).

No saint could come close to St Nicholas however, and though his cult waned in areas, pockets such as Holland stayed firm. For years Dutch men would flock to harbour festivals on St Nicholas' Day, then merrily return home via "Nicholas fairs" buying treats for their children.

The combination of treats, gifts, and discipline meant St Nick was popular among both children and parents, as good behaviour could be encouraged through the year with a few choice words about what might happen in December. And if you've got both children and parents on side, you've got a tradition to last for generations.

THE FIRST ENGLISH CHRISTMASES

The church had an ongoing battle with St Nicholas (and still does) – one of their own saints somehow grown out of control. Wherever the church reached, there was stubborn pagan worship that didn't like to be shifted.

Augustine of Canterbury arrived in England (settling, quite by chance, in Canterbury) not long after Christianity did, and on Christmas Day 597 he baptized 10,000 Saxons in Kent. Mass Christmas baptisms were common, but the challenges for the new converts were just beginning. They had a different route to their faith than their southern European counterparts before them. The Romans had fun popular festivals to build on, and had lived alongside independent Christians first. They had seen Christianity grow from a persecuted underground movement to the official state religion, while in Britain and Northern Europe, they liked their old customs. Just as the Romans weren't keen to drop their Saturnalia and Kalends, the Anglo-Saxons weren't going to drop their animal sacrifices in a hurry.

Pope Gregory the Great wrote to Augustine in 601, advising that he shouldn't seek to replace pagan custom, but absorb it. By the time Christmas arrived in Britain, it's likely that Yule had got there first, or at least many of its customs. So rather than sacrifice animals to old gods, or sometimes even the devil, the locals were encouraged to perform the same actions for the Christian God.

By 700, we're told by St Bede that "the Angli began the year on 25 December when we celebrate the birth of the Lord; and that very night which we hold so sacred, they called in their tongue 'Modranecht'. That is, 'mother's night'." This mother was not Mary, but linked to earlier pagan worship and possibly Yule – but a maternal festival surely made Nativity's takeover a little easier.

Christmas had certainly arrived in Britain, though it would be some centuries before it would take over Easter as the more popular event. The British Christmas was ready for the long game though – over the next 1,200 years it would make such a home, it would alter celebrations across the world.

Three Christmas Day baptisms...

✧ 496: King Clovis I is baptized with 3,000 of his Franks, following a military victory.

✧ 597: Augustine baptizes more than 10,000 Kentish Saxons. With assistance.

✧ 2006: The daughter of Ben Affleck and Jennifer Garner. Granted, it was Christmas Eve, and it's no 10,000 Saxons, but it's still worth reporting. Alright, I just needed a third.

O TANNENBAUM

It wasn't just Britain where there was an ongoing tension between Christianity and pagan custom. One hurdle for Christian missionaries was the Yule log – not easy to skip over. Tree worship had been popular since its Norse nature-worshipping origins, and it proved difficult to convince the locals otherwise.

Oak trees were particularly worshipped. Rather than do away with all tree worship, the church encouraged just shifting over to one tree – the fir. As an evergreen, it was the perfect seasonal fit – plus its triangular shape gave it a good representation of the Trinity.

Perhaps the clincher for some new recruits was that one point of the triangle represented the Holy Spirit. So what if a few of those early converts thought that, in a way, they were still worshipping some kind of holy tree spirit? These things take time.

One story tells of St Boniface of Crediton, an English missionary in eighth-century Germany. Boniface stumbled upon a human sacrifice in a forest clearing – a boy was strapped to an oak tree for the ceremony in worship to Odin. The missionary cut down the oak tree in anger, preventing the sacrifice. As he faced the angry pagans, in place of the felled oak there grew a small fir tree in its place, a symbol of new faith over old. They saw and believed – as did many who heard the story. It would be a while before the Christmas tree would catch on, and a long time before it was brought inside, but perhaps this tale helped ensure that when it was brought inside, it was a fir.

"WASSAILE THE TREES, THAT THEY MAY BEARE, YOU MANY A PLUM AND MANY A PEAR..."

Old England too was in love with its trees (anyone who's been to a National Trust property can testify we still are). Again, the church's plans for Christmas were slightly different to the locals' ideas, so while the Twelve Days of Christmas were meant to bookend Western and Eastern dates of Christmas, England had another idea. Back in the late first millennium it was still little more than a time to reflect on the changing season, and now that the winter solstice had passed, the days were getting longer and farmers hoped for the swift return of their crops.

In the west of England on "Old Twelvy Night", farmers would celebrate with a "wes hal" – Old English for "good health". At the turn of the first millennium, "Wassail!" was the equivalent utterance to "Cheers!", to be responded to with a hearty "Drinkhail!" The wassailing tradition was a crucial part of the farming calendar, and not just because drink and song maketh a mighty fine party. It was more about hopes for harvest and harking back to nature worship. Much of the cider wouldn't be consumed (although much would), instead being daubed on the oldest apple tree in the orchard, with cries of "Awake from your sleep, tree!"

There would be a Wassail Queen, crowned with the ivy, mistletoe, and lichen that were so beloved of Britain's early druids. Songs would be sung, blessings would be pronounced, and cider would be raised to the trees, seemingly dead but possibly resting. One reveller would wear the mask of a bull as a symbol of fertility. Bread or salt would be placed in the fork of the tree's branches, and the tree would be sprinkled with cider. Perhaps this fine drink, made with apples from this tree a season ago, could revive the tree into life for another year? When it did, it meant that the circle of life had delivered once more.

The wassail bowl had ancient origins: to drink communally from one bowl shows equality – and a lack of poison. The Christian communion bonds with similar trust. Though wassails may have fallen out of favour, they still exist as part of rural Christmases today, as of course do the many toasts of wine and... well, pretty much every other alcoholic beverage that sits in my cupboard untouched year-round. Anyone for an out-of-date Baileys?

These traditions were a core part of English culture (an apple core indeed). In the ninth century, King of Wessex Alfred the Great decreed that the Twelve Days of Christmas should be set aside for celebration. No work was to be done – just plenty of wassailing. As for royal plans for a gluttonous boozy Christmas? They were just getting started.

The Frolic of My Lord of Misrule at the Feast of Fools.
The Lord of Misrule was an officer appointed by lot, or
the drawing of lots, at Christmas to preside over the
Feast of Fools. From the Century edition of Cassell's
Illustrated History of England, published 1901

Chapter 4

Merrie Olde England

(935–1588)

It took till the eleventh century before Christ's festival – "Cristes Maesse" – was finally called "Christmas". By now it had become Europe's most prominent religious festival and, like the Roman festivals before it, it had grown from one day to many. From Martinmas and Advent, through Christmastide and the twelve days, onto Epiphany and ultimately Candlemas, the focus was less on the day and more on the season. Plenty of time for a right royal feast.

England's kings led from the front in rebranding this a season for overindulgence. In this chapter, we'll delve into a few of these extravagant royal feasts. The poor of course enjoyed humbler fare: a simpler domestic Christmas of Mass, Christmas pies, and a burning Yule log. They might even be obliged to give a Christmas gift to their king.

In this festival of gift-giving, there was giving and receiving at all levels, and wealthy landowners were obliged to lay on food and entertainment for their tenants. I laid on a feast once – got food all over my clothes, never invited back.

GOOD KING VÁCLAV

One ruler noted for his charity was Václav the Good, also known as Duke Wenceslaus I of Bohemia. Though only a duke, he was posthumously declared a king after his martyrdom in 935. In life he was a generous ruler who saw the Christmas season as an opportunity to bless widows and orphans with alms.

Soon after his demise, Czech hymns were sung of his legendary care for the poor. Today his only link to our festive season is the poem that became a St Stephen's Day carol – not a Christmas carol, but St Stephen's Day is only one day after Christmas, so "Good King Wenceslas" remains in our Christmas culture today.

WILLIAM I

Across Europe, William the Conqueror made his Christmas donation not to the poor but to the Pope, in Christmas 1067. William had always felt that Christmas offered particular blessings, especially to him. He was one of several who opted for Christmas Day as their coronation day – a double celebration. It had the desired effect, though unfortunately caused so much raucous cheering that guards outside Westminster Abbey thought the king was being attacked. They rushed to break up the rabble, killing many in the crowd and setting a few houses on fire.

His subsequent Christmases were formal, relatively calm occasions, with elaborate tableware and endless courses. High-ranking guests ate roast beef at top table, while lower-ranking guests ate boiled meat on a plate made of stale bread. Having a plate you could eat certainly saved on washing up. The poorer still might have been lucky enough to get some scraps from the king's plate, which he majestically slopped out afterwards.

Ten Christmas coronations...

✧ 333: Emperor Constantine anoints his youngest son Constans to become a Caesar (which was a rank rather than a confusing name-change).

✧ 800: Charlemagne crowned Holy Roman Emperor. Almost every European living today is a descendant of Charlemagne – he had at least eighteen children by several wives and concubines. (I'm delighted to tell you that I've done the research: I'm Charlemagne's great-(x41) grandson. You may call me Your Highness.)

✧ 855: Edmund Martyr crowned king of East Anglia at a ceremony in Suffolk.

✧ 1025: Mieszko II Lambert crowned king of Poland.

✧ 1066: William the Conqueror crowned King William I of England at Westminster Abbey. There is much rejoicing/ killing.

✧ 1076: Boleslaw II the Generous crowned king of Poland. He was so-named because he built many churches. Boleslaw's brother Coleslaw was so-named because he liked cabbage salad in mayonnaise (not true).

✧ 1100: Baldwin of Boulogne crowned as first king of Jerusalem. The coronation took place on Christmas Day in Bethlehem, at the Church of the Nativity, winning the prize for the Christmassiest coronation ever.

✧ 1130: Count Roger II crowned first king of Sicily.

✧ 1559: Pope Pius IV elected.

✧ 1926: Prince Hirohito becomes emperor of Japan, though the date was not his choice – he assumed the title on the death of his father Emperor Taishō.

HENRYS I AND II

In 1125, William's son Henry I had a special Christmas gift for those who had debased his currency: vengeance. All the country's mint-men were invited to Winchester; by Twelfth Night, all were deprived of their right hands and their, er… – well, they may have literally made money, but they left with no family jewels.

Henry II was crowned a week before Christmas in 1154; four years later on Christmas Day, he removed his crown, placed it on the altar, and never wore it again. We've all taken party crowns off on Christmas Day (often because the paper rips) – Henry II did it and kept reigning for another thirty-one years. Perhaps he just found his a bit itchy.

Christmas Day 1170 was a notorious landmark for Henry. In the French town of Bure, he famously uttered dissatisfaction with his Archbishop of Canterbury, Thomas Becket. Whether or not Henry actually declared, "Who will rid me of this turbulent priest?", the result was that four days later, Becket had been murdered. Careful what you mutter about any slightly annoying friends this Christmas.

One year later we find the grandest feast of Henry's reign. In Dublin in December 1171, Henry shocked his Irish hosts with the sheer size and scale consumed by his travelling court. He had every alcoholic drink imaginable: wine, mead, claret, ale, cider, and hypocras, a honeyed wine. The birds served at dinner included swan, peacock, and most controversially crane. The Irish noblemen refused to eat it; Henry insisted – tuck in.

The after-dinner entertainment featured dwarf-tossing and Henry's legendary jester Roland le Pettour (Roland "the Farter"), lured out of retirement for his famous "leap, whistle, and fart" routine. It sounds a lot more cultured in Latin – *saltum, siffletum, et pettum*. How sad that no recording is available of Roland's legendary performance, though a royal Christmas 200 years later hosted the harmonic farting of minstrels, so maybe that's due a comeback.

KING JOHN

By now, the Christmas season was shrinking again. It had enjoyed a longer run through Advent up to Twelfth Night – but that's a long time to take off work, so come on citizens, no slacking.

Religious observances were still kept: Advent was traditionally a time of fasting, with that fast being broken at Christmas when the feasting could begin. King John certainly made up for that lost time. He was observed in Caen, France during Christmas 1202 "faring sumptuously every day and prolonging his morning slumbers until dinner time". Sounds like the Christmases of my teenage years, personally.

John's 1213 banquet considerably upped the game, by serving everything from peacock to, well, game. John was born on Christmas Eve 1166, exactly 100 years after William the Conqueror's dual Christmas-plus-coronation party. Inspired by his great-grandfather, John doubled up too. Each Christmas his birthday banquet was a feast for all, wherever he was in the land (John was a rather itinerant king).

We could pick one of many royal banquets for our next date that changed Christmas, but we'll plump for this one, because we happen to have a feast of information about John's new heights of overindulgence…

On our fourth date of Christmas…
(Windsor, 25 December 1213)

King John cordially invites you to a celebration of Christmas, and His Majesty's birthday.

The feast has been weeks in the planning, due to the sheer scale of what is to be served. The moment that His Majesty decided he would be Christmassing at Windsor Castle, the local sheriff was charged with sourcing the goods, causing much commotion for miles around as suppliers were drained of their stocks. Who among us can forget 1206's Christmas in Winchester, when the Sheriff of Hampshire was given ten days to find 1,500 hens, 5,000 eggs, 20 cattle, 100 pigs, and 100 sheep? The Sheriff of Wiltshire was roped in to help find half a kilometre of linen tablecloth.

This Christmas is no exception. The king's trusted chief official Reginald de Cornhill has been tasked with ordering the following:

> 24 hogsheads of ordinary wine (each hogshead holds between sixty and ninety gallons. They aren't actual hogs' heads…)
> 420 pigs' heads (oh, these are actual hogs' heads…)
> 16,000 hens
> Partridges and pheasants – as many as can be found
> 50lb pepper
> 2lb saffron
> 100lb almonds
> 15,000 herrings
> 10,000 salted eels
> 500lb of wax for candles
> Plus cloves, nutmeg, cinnamon, and ginger spices, fresh from the Crusades

… aah, that even smells like Christmas. No one goes hungry here, including the poor, who will benefit from leftovers and handouts. Noblemen will be granted new and excellent robes as is the custom. (For how else will anyone know that the king's finances are doing well? Knights of the land riding around in fresh garments is the only way, of course!)

The new Archbishop of Canterbury is rumoured to have procured himself extra robes to additionally dole out to his closest men. Sounds to me like a dangerous game of one-upmanship, given what's happened to previous archbishops with one Christmas murmur from the king (cough Thomas Becket cough).

PEACOCK PIE

A shopping list like this fed the court for several days. The idea was to have different foods each day: a goose with saffron one meal, roasted swan the next, or maybe peacock pie. Peacock was known to be rather dry and not particularly pleasant – but nothing looked more magnificent. Its head would stick out of one end of the pie, the tail at the other. Because of its toughness, often the head and tail were the only bits of peacock in attendance. The meat inside might actually be far tastier goose or chicken.

Like the pie, John soon discovered what it was like to have little of his inner circle in attendance. While his typical banquets were vast, John dined alone at Christmas 1214, on a collision course with his barons that would lead to the Magna Carta soon after. It goes to show: be nice to your underlings, at Christmas and through the year – otherwise you'll need a nice big card to say sorry.

THE BOAR'S HEAD

Boar was a popular centrepiece, served at royal feasts with a lemon or apple in its mouth and garnished with rosemary and bay leaves. An equivalent was popular down the ranks too, with pickled pigs' ears and trotters being served with cheese and apples, perhaps with mutton filling out the plate.

Although the wild boar was hunted to extinction during the Middle Ages, the "Boar's Head Carol" lasted far longer than the beast itself. The carol would be sung to welcome this noted dish, but even without musical accompaniment there was a certain ritual to serving the boar. It harked back to our Norse friends, known to sacrifice the boar to seek blessings from the god Freyr. The boar was seen as sovereign of the forest. Therefore conquering the beast, as well as harnessing the fruit, was man being victorious over nature, while nervously requesting that the gods provide again next year.

There have been efforts to Christianize or anglicize the backstory. One belief was that the presentation of the boar represented Christ's triumph over sin; a separate origin story had an Oxford philosophy student meeting an angry boar on the way to Midnight Mass, before ramming his philosophy book down the beast's throat to escape a mauling.

There are still boar's head customs in parts of England at Christmases today – it's even suggested that this is the oldest continuing festivity of the Christmas season. For the most part though, boar's head traditions have waned, if only relatively recently. The joint of ham served at the start of Christmas dinner is all that remains at many Christmas tables – and in recent years, even that ham has gone the way of the dodo (dodo was never served at Christmas dinner… that I know of).

MINCE PIES... WITH REAL MINCE

For many in the twenty-first century, one of the most recognizable facets of Christmas is the food. It simply wouldn't be Christmas without the Christmas pudding, or the mince pies, or the turkey, or all the trimmings. But the medieval kings ate many meats alien to most of us (just imagine – roasted alien…), as most of our modern foodstuffs were yet to come.

Mince pies were just starting to come in, though not as we know them. Their pies had genuine meat. Since Roman days, the mixing of savoury meat with sweet foods was a delicacy. These sweetmeat pies now had a new addition: spices from the Crusades, so now they could be extra sweet – and extra meaty. They were rectangular rather than round – the circular mince pie had a good reason for its reinvention, which we'll find out around the time of Cromwell. For now though, these "coffin" pies were thought to imitate Jesus' crib. Crib or coffin then? The theologically minded might like it to reflect both.

HENRY III

John's son Henry III kept the family traditions going, eating vastly but also sharing the spoils. He gave significant Christmas gifts to the church to curry favour with God. In 1241 he gave gifts to Westminster Abbey, including new gold-laced vestments and expensive silks. Oh, he gave his wife a gift too. And in case you're ever stuck on what to buy royalty, five Christmases earlier, the king of France gave King Henry a live elephant.

At Christmas 1248, Westminster Hall was filled, and not by the elephant. Impoverished diners were treated to a full week of full stomachs, at the expense of the king.

1251's feast was Henry III's biggest that we know of. This Christmas coincided with the wedding of his daughter, at the age of eleven. Her husband, the king of Scotland, had just turned ten – clearly he was drawn to the older lady (it's encouraging to hear that they waited to consummate the marriage, although only till they were both fourteen).

The Christmas/wedding banquet included 70 pigs, 1,000 cod, 500 conga eels, 10,000 haddock, 1,992 hens (how specific), 1,600 partridges, 120 peacocks, 290 pheasants, 300 rabbits, 125 swans… and that was just for starters. Well it may not have been just for starters, but there was plenty more ordered too.

The extravagances were not going unnoticed. One guest, Benedictine monk Matthew of Paris, noted at the time: "The worldly and wanton vanity of the scene, if it were to be described in full, would produce wonder and weariness in those who heard it."

THAT'S EDWARDTAINMENT...

New traditions crept in, in the only way they could – by being royally sanctioned. Kings Edward I and Edward III were particularly influential in the realms of regal entertainment.

Edward I encouraged dressing up at Christmas, requesting that his lords and ladies wear fancy silk finery for an Arthurian-themed dinner at a specially constructed round table. Once again, Christmas couldn't help looking to the past to see how to celebrate today. For Edward, his noblemen were to be entertained and the poor fed; at Christmas in 1283 he ensured that 500 London beggars had Christmas dinner.

Sixty years later, Edward III was so taken with King Arthur's legend that he created a brand new chivalrous order at Christmas – "the Order of the Garter". His love of entertainment gave us one of our most persistent Christmas entertainments, still celebrated in some British pubs today: the mummers' play.

Such brash tales of good versus evil aren't at the heart of our Christmases as they used to be. These festive farces have been replaced by home entertainment, TV specials, and family-friendly theatre shows: mumming's own direct descendants. From pantomime to extended sitcom episodes to celebrity gameshows, these light-hearted seasonal plays-for-laughs are mummers' plays in disguise – and disguise was something mumming knew all about. Seek them out, you can still find them today.

Seven observations from my pub's mummers' play
(COURTESY OF *THE PILGRIM MORRIS MEN* AT *THE KEEP PUB*, GUILDFORD ON 6 JANUARY 2017)...

✦   *WASSAILS NOT JANUARY SALES...* The High Street may look like a commercial jungle, but look to the pubs and you'll find the community. They vary nationwide, but in the Surrey town of Guildford, the mummers' play tours five pubs each Twelfth Night, a half-hour performance in each. Most pub-goers have no clue what's about to happen; in ours, a policeman thinks his retirement party has booked it all just for him.

✧ *VERY FANCY DRESS…* In the summer, they're Morris dancers; in midwinter, they're mummers. Replete with rainbow-coloured costumes, from Mad Hatter to a green Father Christmas, dozens of dressed-up (often well-oiled) wassailers fill the pub. It's a health and safety nightmare: sloshing alcohol, flammable costumes, the odd candle, a packed pub… in fact many can't fit in and shiver outside like the little match girl – but at least they'll be first in the next pub.

✧ *PANTO MEETS PUB CRAWL…* Most are following rather than performing, but they sing heartily and quaff from tankards they've brought specially. Ours is their second pub of the night, and some stops have variations. The first pub, The Star, saw the Twelfth Cake shared out; I'm told that Colin found a bean in his slice, crowning him Colin II, King of Misrule for the next few hours. The third pub features extended carolling, and I get the impression that by the fifth pub, The Royal Oak, the play will have evolved from The Star's sober performance.

✧ *DRINKHAIL!…* The wassail bowl is passed around. I of course take a sip, much to the eye-rolling of my wife, already fearing whatever seasonal virus we'll all share, before she takes a drink too.

◈ *I KNOW THIS ONE…* The half-hour pop-up performance is like an ancient flashmob, opened, closed, and middled with carols. Some have familiar words, some do not. None have familiar tunes. Yet the regular mummers (some of whom may have enjoyed eighty or more Old Twelvy Nights) don't waver. By the eighth or ninth verse, I nail the tune too. I couldn't sing "As I Sat on a Sunny Bank" to any other tune now. I'm surprised to see so much Christian tradition: even unfamiliar carols feature Jesus and Mary, as well as yes, holly, ivy, the wassail bowl, and a maid in a lily-white smock. Oh my.

◈ *ANCIENT AND MODERN…* The wassailing shows no signs of waning. Smartphones and our love of tech may keep many of us at home, but we still crave community. As we sing, selfies are taken, group photos are posted to Instagram, and there's the joyous sight of a face-painted, bearded seventy-year-old in tinsel hat and outlandish outfit, reading the half-millennium-old "Boar's Head Carol" from his illuminated iPad.

◈ *THE PLAY'S THE THING…* As for the play itself, like all mummers' plays it's a variation on a theme. The words may change, but the characters and loose storyline are pretty much the same. Overacting is essential, cheers and jeers from the crowd are encouraged, and if you can see or hear what's going on then that's a bonus (or not, depending on the acting). I'll be there again next year. ~~Cheers!~~ Wassail!

MUMMING FOR DUMMIES

How better to explain what the plays are about, than present a new one. So here's my mummers' play guide to mummers' plays, or at least how they used to be, back when men were men, and also women, thanks to wigs, dresses, and medieval misogyny:

MUMMERS:

> *A carol's sung by all to start*
> *Before they go to play their part.*
> *No stage as such, they simply stood*
> *On floor of pub, or else they would*
> *Go house-to-house, in great disguise,*
> *No warning or knocking – just "Surprise!"*
> *No actresses performed, just actors,*
> *Still called "mummers"; no, not "dadders".*
> *Mumming's named from silent "mime"*
> *Though yes, they spoke, and yes, in rhyme.*
> *The Fool narrates in most productions,*
> *Mostly with this introduction…*

FOOL:

> *I open the door, I enter in,*
> *I hope your favour we shall win.*
> *Stir up the fire and strike a light,*
> *And see my merry boys act tonight.*
> *Whether we stand or whether we fall,*
> *We'll do our best to please you all!*
> *(Then each who enters, says the same:*
> *"In comes I…" and then their name…)*

ST GEORGE:

*In comes I – St George! And now I'll boast of how I'm bold,
I'll wave around my sword and shield, and wear a crown of
gold.
You'll all have heard my big success in taking on a dragon,
So drink to victories gone by – Come on, now raise your
flagon!*

KING OF EGYPT:

*In comes I, the King of Egypt. George! My son and heir!
None shall ever vanquish you, especially him o'er there.*

TURKISH KNIGHT:

*In comes I, a Turkish Knight named Slasher – yes, I know…
Political correctness wasn't common long ago.
After all, we've always loved a tale of good v evil,
Crusades weren't long before, so this is why it roused the
people.*

ST GEORGE:

*A-ha! Some swordplay now ensues; I'll stab the Knight, now
die!*

TURKISH KNIGHT:

Urgh!…

FOOL: …

Another character will mourn the knight, and cry.

KING OF EGYPT:

*"Oh Slasher, friend and chum! I can't believe you're dead," I'll
blub.*

FOOL:

> *Fear not! I'll ask, "Is there a doctor in the house?" (or pub?)*

ST GEORGE:

> *But don't you see, you Fool, the Turkish Knight is proper slain!*

FOOL:

> *Ah yes, but don't you know that in these plays he lives again?*
> *One common notion in these plays: the resurrecting victim.*
> *Spring buds forth from winter! Doesn't matter that you pricked him.*
> *Another frequent factor is the healer's out for money,*
> *This Quackish Doctor now comes on: perennially funny.*

QUACKISH DOCTOR:

> *Did someone seek a doctor? What you paying?*

KING OF EGYPT:

> *What's your rate?*

QUACKISH DOCTOR:

> *Usually it's fifteen quid, for you, I'll escalate.*
> *So call it twenty...*

KING OF EGYPT:

> *Twenty pounds?!*

QUACKISH DOCTOR:

> *...Thirty! Final offer!*

KING OF EGYPT:

> *Alright, be quick, you quack, and make him better – fill your*
> *coffers!*

FOOL:

> *The doctor works his magic, Slasher's better – All will cheer!*
> *Then plenty other characters will probably appear:*
> *A horse! Beelzebub! And (crucially for books like this)*
> *In later years the Fool would be replaced by Father*
> *Christmas.*

OLD FATHER CHRISTMAS:

> *In come I, old Father Christmas,*
> *Welcome or welcome not.*
> *I hope old Father Christmas*
> *Will never be forgot.*

FOOL:

> *From 1600s on, these words were always used when*
> *mumming,*
> *'Cos Christmas would be banned: that's a story we've got*
> *coming.*
> *The end of every mummers' play was Little Johnny Jack,*
> *The poorest character of all, with bags upon his back.*

LITTLE JOHNNY JACK:

> *In comes Little Johnny Jack, to ask the folks for food,*
> *And then I'd ask for money – and they'd give, unless they're*
> *rude.*
> *For all this entertainment, this traditional jolly fable,*
> *At end of play, and end of day, means food upon our table.*

OLD MAN WINTER

The text of the earliest such plays is sadly lost to us, but the ongoing performances show local differences. Some areas feature Snap the Dragon, The 'Owd 'Oss, or The Derby Tup (all animals, a.k.a. cloth-carrying men snapping jaws with a pole). Some call it "guising", "mumming", "mumping", "gusards", or "Thomasing", for St Thomas' Day.

The Yule crossover is clear: revival of nature, spring through winter. Old Father Christmas grew out of "Old Winter", a character completely separate from any notion of St Nicholas or Santa Claus. As for the character of Summer – well you'll have to watch Australian soap operas for that.

Old Man Winter was probably inherited by merry England from the Norse culture. Any similarity to our images of St Nick would have been because of the white beard, but otherwise there was little in common – Old Winter was no generous giver of gifts. Instead he was a passive character, welcomed in from the cold and appeased with food and ale. Be nice to Old Winter, he might give way to New Spring soon.

By the mid-fifteenth century, there were figures portrayed not just as "Winter" but as "Christmas". Reverend Richard Smart of Plymtree in Devon was the earliest to reference a "Sir Christèmas", who declares news of Christ's birth. If modern versions of Santa have veered from the Christian side of Christmas, it's worth remembering that the earliest version of Father Christmas heralded the Nativity.

THE NEW SATURNALIA?

These plays had been informally performed for years, but Edward III's first royal command performance in 1347 gave him a taste for them, and for more raucous celebrations. The following year he spent Halloween to Candlemas – three full months – on a Saturnalia-themed Christmas in my own home town of Guildford. There were costumes and masks for eighty people, with animal skins and cross-dressing (as a resident, I can report it's not changed much in 700 years).

In Christmas 1377, the ten-year-old King Richard II was treated to a full "Mummers' Parade". Over 100 Londoners guised themselves as knights and cardinals and marched through the city, ending at the young king's residence in Kennington. Here they pretended to gamble against the king with dice, shrewdly always letting him win.

Richard thanked Christmas for his divine royal appointment: he was born on 6 January, the day of the visit of the Magi. His birth was even witnessed by three kings: of Castille, Navarre, and Portugal.

As he grew, he continued that fine tradition of gastronomic extravagance. He hosted King Leon of Armenia in 1386, and was eager to demonstrate just how the English feasted. Twenty-eight oxen, 300 sheep, thousands of birds, and twelve days later, 10,000 bellies left Eltham Palace a little bloated.

FRUMENTY

An early cookbook from the 1390s has been very helpful in seeing what was cooked for these feasts. "The Forme of Cury" includes the recipe for a festive favourite that would last centuries, and be known as England's oldest national dish: frumenty.

This spiced porridge was of Celtic origin, making it about as British as food could get. It was originally made to appease the harvest god, Dagda, with the whole family giving it a stir to show their faith. When the religious element fell away, it became a favourite at year-round dinners – frumenty isn't just for

Christmas, but for other celebration days including Mothering Sunday and even local sheep-shearing customs.

A mixture of ingredients including cracked wheat, almonds, currants, milk, eggs, raisins, and various fish and meat were stirred in a cauldron of boiling water, and at noble feasts it might even be served in a tableau as part of a castle or hunting scene.

STIR-UP SUNDAY

Years on, frumenty would change into plum porridge (not necessarily with plum, but with generic fruit), then the very popular plum pudding. Lose the meat and fish, and it resembles our modern Christmas pudding.

One way of making it was to cook it in a wrapped cloth, forming a ball. Over the years this cloth vanished, and half of that ball was left and became our simple pudding basin. And that stirring custom for the harvest god Dagda? That would become "Stir-up Sunday", still a tradition in many families today, on the last Sunday before Advent. The 1549 Book of Common Prayer ties the occasion in with the words of that day's collect: "Stir up, we beseech thee, O Lord, the wills of thy faithful people…"

The mixture is stirred east to west, mimicking the sun, which is also symbolized in the flame. The holly on top is a nod to those pre-Christian origins, plus a Roman element: the coin inside our Christmas pudding was originally a bean, and whoever had it would be appointed "King of the Bean", or "Lord of Misrule", whether in ancient days under Roman emperors, or in my present-day pub under Colin II. To Christianize this popular pud, it's now said that it was made with thirteen ingredients, representing the twelve disciples and Jesus, though it's a combination of many elements of Christmas over the years: Norse, Roman, Celtic, and Christian.

TOO MUCH?

The banquets may have grown in size, but they were not messy or raucous. By the time of Edward IV in the late fifteenth century, courtesy books explained etiquette to any not in the know. They were hierarchical, civilized affairs. High-ranking officials had the privilege of serving the king – even carving or testing the food were jobs delegated to noblemen. The mumming continued, but there were also political dramas, and reports of less highbrow entertainment such as jumping out of a cake.

By now though, there were murmurings that these expansive feasts may have grown a little out of control, especially when the purse of the kingdom was a little light. One historical chronicler, a monk, observed of one of Richard III's celebrations that: "During this feast of the Nativity, far too much attention was given to dancing and gaiety."

One feature of the gaiety was the aforementioned Lord of Misrule. Henry VII's Christmas of 1489 featured a particularly notable version of this – though the tradition's days were numbered.

LORD OF MISRULE AND THE BOY BISHOP

The Abbot of Unreason, the King of the Bean, the Captain of Mischief, the Lord of Misrule – whatever you called him, he'd grown little since Roman days. A peasant would be elected or chosen by lot to rule the festivities, from quizzing with riddles (with minor punishments if you answered wrong) to dictating games of Blind Man's Buff or the ill-advised Snapdragon (snatching raisins from flaming brandy). The mock monarch would sit on the high table in ill-fitting gowns, as servants exaggerated gestures of subservience to their temporary master.

It was the nearest the Middle Ages had to irony, though the whole charade was far from subtle. Drunkenness, naughtiness, and a dose of anarchy followed the Lord everywhere. He wouldn't just command dancing or drinking, he would cause chaos – prancing into a church service mid-sermon for example, jangling the bells attached to his legs and waving his coloured handkerchiefs. Imagine a Morris dancer invading a quiet bit on *Songs of Praise*. Awkward, isn't it?

The church had their take on this, called the Boy Bishop. Their more sober and solemn version focused on the topsy-turvy nature of the season, present ever since Saturnalia. While the Lord of Misrule reigned from Halloween to Candlemas (31 October to 2 February), the church's child equivalent ruled between the church's two key dates for children: from St Nicholas Day on 6 December to Holy Innocents Day (more catchily named "Childermas") on 28 December, the day commemorating Herod's Massacre of the Innocents. Once elected, the Boy Bishop would replace the real bishop, sitting in his seat and dressed in full mitre and robes. He would perform all church ceremonies except Mass – even delivering sermons, while the regular clergy took on junior tasks.

This was no parody though – the atmosphere was sombre, and if there was any levity in the sermons, it was droll humour written by the adult clergy. Still it was a popular annual event, although some thought it undermined the church. The related "Feast of Fools" was similarly anarchic – generally on New Year's Day, lower clergy and peasants dressed up as animals, women, or their superiors.

We can see the influence of Roman culture, how this event appeased those lower down the social ladder – but its heathen origins had little place in the church, with seeds of Reformation sprouting in Europe. The Council of Basle abolished the customs in the fifteenth century, and Henry VIII banned them in England by 1541. The more secular Lord of Misrule was a favourite of Henry's though; this seasonal joker had his pay doubled over a few years. As a jobbing comedian I can tell you this is unheard of.

Henry's Christmases were typically grand with great pageantry. In his early reign, one Christmas dinner featured "an abundance of viands as hath beene few times seene", including venison, peacock, swan, porpoise, seagull, and heron – the more exotic the better! It's alleged that the Duke of Northumberland ate five swans that Christmas. Do that today, and you'd get looks.

FOWL!

Tudor roast dinners looked increasingly similar to ours. Root vegetables were eaten nearly as much as meat and newcomers like sprouts were joining the plate. These perennial "favourites" (personally I still have to gulp my one-sprout-a-year down with a glass of red) offered highly nutritious vitamins through the season, unusually growing in even the roughest of winters.

New foodstuffs arrived in the hand luggage of explorers. Sugar was an expensive luxury but helpful for the traditional Christmas sweetmeats; sugared bacon was a Tudor delicacy. But the prized souvenir was a meat, because after all, a special occasion such as Christmas deserves a special bird – and goose, swan, and peacock had all been done.

The Southern Mexican turkey was a domesticated bird, making it very easy to transport, so by 1525 these birds started appearing in European ports. Originally it was confused with the African guinea fowl, arriving via the Ottoman empire, land of the Turks. So the turkey suffered a case of mistaken identity; though it had never even been to Turkey, the name "turkey" stuck.

The whole naming of this bird is one giant fiasco, to be honest. The country it was thought to be from wasn't even called Turkey until after World War I, so the bird was (wrongly) named first. Then there's the fact that the bird they thought it was wasn't even from Turkey (which wasn't called Turkey) but East Africa – the birds just changed hands a few times between Turks en route. Finally, the world over, they all seem to call it different names based on other places that *it's not even from*. The Turks themselves called it "an Indian bird", as did the French who call it an "Indian rooster" (a "*coq d'Inde*", now abridged to "*dinde*"). In Malaysia it's a "Dutch chicken", while the Portuguese call it a "Peru bird". The humble turkey should really be called "Mexican guinea fowl lookalike".

Yorkshireman William Strickland bought six turkeys from some Native Americans and brought them to British shores via the Spanish Netherlands; the first turkeys were sold in Bristol at the price of tuppence – unsurprisingly at that rate, the locals gobbled them up.

MOTHER GOOSE

But this was at least a two-bird race to the dinner plate. The goose was faring well as a seasonal bird to eat, just not necessarily at Christmas. Instead Michaelmas on 29 September was the day that each goose should look over its shoulders. They'd been popular with the Celts in their Samhain festival and also in our very old friend Yule.

Long before the Dutch/American/Mexican/Peruvian/Indian turkey could get its claws onto our Christmas menu, the goose beat it to it. This was all thanks to another sea explorer, not bringing anything back from the New World but defending the Old World. Sir Francis Drake and Lord Charles Howard led the defence against the Spanish Armada, and on 29 September 1588 word reached Queen Elizabeth of their success. She was tucking into her traditional Michaelmas goose at the time, and was so overjoyed at the victory that she decreed that goose become celebration food from then on. That Christmas, roasted goose was the bird of choice. So when Michaelmas later declined, the goose clung to Christmas instead. In the next century though, James I preferred turkey to boar's head, so the goose's old rival was back on the table. Then in the Victorian era, popular Prince Albert began a fashion (for those who could afford it) for the more succulent turkey – and the goose's goose was cooked.

Locals didn't necessarily have the kitchen equipment to cook their traditional Christmas bird, whether goose, turkey, or snipe (for the poor, it would be goose – money doesn't grow on Christmas trees). So to help everyone enjoy their Christmas dinner, communal ovens were available on Christmas Day, often in bakeries otherwise closed for the day.

BACK TO BASICS

While we've mostly stayed in England in this chapter, we've drifted from a religious Christmas into this all-too-recognizable banquet of gluttony and spectacle. This seemingly modern moan of Christmas becoming a season of excess is perhaps not so modern. English monarchs knew how to throw a Christmas party, but the Puritan government was waiting in the wings to put an end to the monarchy, for a while at least, and to Christmas excess.

Before we see what happens when you ban Christmas (spoiler: not everyone's happy), let's spin back to what was happening in Europe while King John was ordering those extra 16,000 hens. While English kings gorged, Europe was ushering in tinsel, trees, and a second Christmas cave.

Assisi, Umbria. Historic nativity crib scene with
life-size statues, outside of the Church of St Francis

Chapter 5

Caves and Carols

(1181–1610)

If this book is Christmas Day, we're approaching halfway. We've just gorged on more food than is good for us and we've had some ribald entertainment. We even visited the religious place first thing – but that's a while ago now. Between Saturnalia and mumming, was anyone looking to the manger, or were they too busy dining on swan and peacock and frumenty? This chapter sees us glance back to the Nativity and hear the first carols. And forget the royals at the top of the tree – we'll look at the working people trying to fell them. Oh yes, there'll be trees too.

Socially, England at large was celebrating Christmas in name but Yule in spirit, as royal courts overflowed with midwinter feasting and japery. But spiritually, churchgoers were singing a different tune.

Nativity hymns had been sung since the fourth century. For nearly a millennium these were of a similar type: in Latin, based around the incarnation and the holy mother Mary. They were theological in tone and not too descriptive. As the councils decreed on Christ's divinity, these songs reinforced this theology: Jesus as God incarnate, high and mighty rather than lowly and vulnerable. There was scarcely a manger in sight.

SAY WHAT YOU SEE

Once the early church had overcome its uncertainty about celebrating Christ's origin, it began to illustrate it. Stained glass appeared in churches from the fourth and fifth centuries; 100 years later, the Nativity scene would be added to the repertoire of pictures from Christ's life. Mosaics featuring the holy family appeared from the sixth century.

By this time, the Roman conquest of Western Europe was becoming just a memory. Since the Romans' withdrawal, their "vulgar Latin" brought to British common folk seemed like a brief experiment, and had been replaced by Old English. Across Europe, localized languages filled the void. Yet the church doesn't change quickly. Their language was Latin (and in many cases still is), spoken by very few laypeople. Most would have known their Lord's Prayer and Nicene Creed in Latin, but there were no sermons in understandable local vernacular. So those colour illustrations of the life of the Lord they were speaking of would have had an immensely vivid impact. Stained-glass windows may be momentarily diverting to modern eyes, but we shouldn't underestimate their effect on medieval worshippers. It's fair to say that in the twenty-first century, we see more images in one day than our 1,000-year-old ancestors managed in a lifetime.

Three early Nativity plays...

✧   *OFFICIUM PASTORUM* (The Play of the Shepherds)…
     A handful of short plays featuring the shepherds built
     on ninth- and tenth-century Easter plays, known as *The
     Visitatio*. The Abbey of St Martial in Limoges featured
     a drama performed at High Mass on Christmas Day in
     the eleventh century, and there are several versions from
     Rouen. Until the twelfth century, Mary and Joseph were
     played by wooden mannequins.

✧   *OFFICIUM STELLAE* (The Play of the Star)… Far more
     popular were Epiphany plays about the Magi. Three
     priests portrayed the Magi, who were now three kings
     ("…of Orient are, one in a taxi, one in a car…" – such
     additions would be some centuries away, culminating in
     my epic performance at Valley End Infant School in 1983).
     They'd gesture to a star which would appear via a rather
     impressive system of pulleys and ropes, moving across the
     church ceiling to the altar.

✧ *FANCY SEEING YOU HERE…* Alright that wasn't the title but it should have been. By the late twelfth century, the plays merged and shepherds and kings shared the stage. Western Europe now had the Nativity play that we have today – though ours aren't in Latin. For plays in "*lingua franca*" (that's "local language", in local language), we need a bit of assistance – a bit of Assisissistance…

ASSISI AS PIE

St Francis of Assisi was a true custodian of Christmas, with a fascination for language and drama, and particularly how they could be used to give power to the people. He was born Giovanni di Pietro di Bernardone in Assisi, Italy in around 1181, and was swiftly nicknamed "Francesco" by his silk merchant father after some successful business in France. Inspired by an illness, he joined the church, where he grew a passion for working with the homeless. While King John of England was tucking into another Christmas swan, Francis was defiantly living homeless, and even shoeless, alongside Rome's beggars and lepers. He sought papal permission to found a new religious order, which became the Lesser Brothers, or the Franciscan Order. As European knights were fighting in the Crusades, Francis took a diplomatic visit to the Sultan in Egypt, hoping to negotiate a peaceful end to the conflict by converting him to Christianity. The Sultan didn't oblige.

Francis spoke with sultans and popes but was more comfortable with those at street level; the only woman he pledged to marry was "Lady Poverty". He observed the barriers in the way of the poor – including language barriers, which meant changing the way that Jesus' birth was viewed by the layperson. Shifting from sermons on divine incarnation, Francis was inspired by the troubadours he loved as a child; he wanted people to visualize the earthy scene.

In 1220 he was deeply moved by a visit to Jesus' birthplace, the Bethlehem crib seeming as humble and poor as the Rome streets that Francis knew so well. For centuries the people had heard of the divinity of Christ; now it was time to hear of his humanity.

On our fifth date of Christmas...
(Greccio near Assisi, 24 December 1223)

Francis of Assisi presents a first of its kind: a live Christmas Nativity scene – not in a church but in a cave, two miles from the Italian town of Greccio. Permission has been sought from Pope Honorius III, who has given the event his blessing.

The friar intends to change how we view Christmas: "I want to do something that will recall the memory of that Child who was born in Bethlehem, to see with bodily eyes the inconveniences of his infancy, how he lay in the manger, and how the ox and ass stood by."

The animals have been borrowed from the local Lord of Greccio, Giovanni Velita, a former soldier who has joined Francis in renouncing his worldly wealth, though thankfully he's kept at least the ox and ass. Other Franciscan brothers are in attendance, not knowing if any townsfolk will join them when the sun sets. Locals have been invited to bring a lit candle, representing the star over a similar cave twelve centuries before.

Glow by glow, candlelight illuminates the hillside as the crowd climb the path to the cave. Like Francis and his brothers, they object to the secular materialism taking hold in Europe. They seek another way, away from feasting and carnival.

One monk in attendance, St Bonaventure, later writes that Francis presided "with all possible solemnity", not calling Jesus by name but "the Babe of Bethlehem". The manger has real straw and a stone infant; there is no Joseph or Mary but Franciscan brothers are representing shepherds. The real animals and stable setting move the crowd greatly. Many townsfolk live in poverty, and now they see that the Lord they hear of at Mass lived like them too.

Mass is presided over the infant, the manger becoming an altar for bread and wine. Francis sings movingly throughout. Devotion has always been at the core of the Franciscan Order, and though many in attendance are not followers of Francis, they return homeward down the hillside inspired.

EVERY HOME SHOULD HAVE ONE...

The locals spread word of the live Nativity. Numbers grew at the next year's performance, while similar events cropped up across Europe. On smaller scales, crib scenes were carved and sculpted, often with statues wearing real clothes. Soon every church in Italy had a crib scene; many were life-size.

Over the next few hundred years, these crib scenes arrived in houses too. It became quite the thing to recreate the Nativity scene when hosting domestic Christmas parties, often comparing crib scene size. Just as the charity of St Nicholas had grown into materialism, so had the devotion of St Francis grown into seasonal competitiveness.

Francis' legacy was to engage common folk in a way that high theology hadn't before, relating it to the poverty and agriculture so familiar to working Europeans. Each Christmas to this day, Franciscan monks put on a crib scene in that same cave near Greccio.

LOCAL PLAYS FOR LOCAL PEOPLE

St Francis' other legacy stemmed from his passion to connect with people where they were, requiring devotionals and liturgy in their language. Few attended school of any sort, so there was no hope of widespread Latin comprehension beyond those key prayers or creeds – no *amo, amas, amat* here. The people needed to understand what they were saying.

The Franciscans wrote devotional poems in local languages, not just for Christmas but as a chance to engage with the life of Christ through the year, with biblical retellings from the Creation to the Day of Judgment. A papal edict in 1210 had banned the clergy from performing plays in church, meaning that ownership was shifting to the people. With St Francis' encouragement of the local vernacular, monks began to pen plays for local audiences. Humour and elaborate storytelling enthused those who watched. The famous "mystery plays" of Coventry and York grew from these influences, lasting till the Reformation – all stemming from that barefoot friar.

Six lessons about carols...

✧   *BAWDY AND FRENCH...* Carols began in France, not as songs but as dances, and not necessarily to do with Christmas (otherwise why would we call them "Christmas carols"?). They weren't necessarily sacred – in fact they were rather bawdy. Until St Francis, Christmas music stayed well and truly away from church. Religious music was confined to monasteries, because only monks could read music.

✧   *THE MEDIEVAL HOKEY-COKEY...* The church dragged carols from being brash circular dances into use for festivals and processions. Circles became lines.

✧ *WE WON'T GO UNTIL WE'VE GOT SOME…* While the French danced and the church processed, the Anglo-Saxons wassailed. Small choirs would tour the parish, not to spread the church's message, but because they weren't welcome in church until they stopped singing their silly songs. Pure festive escapism.

✧ *KEEP DANCING!…* William of Malmesbury of the twelfth century told an advisory horror story: "Othbert, a sinner" refused to stop dancing his outrageous carols, so was cursed to keep dancing for a full year, till he danced into a deep pit. So, obey the church's instruction, or that could be you, the eternal dancer of carols…

✧ *"HEY, MACARONIC…"* The new non-Latin Christian songs and poems included some that were macaronic – mixing two languages – like 1328's famous "*in dulci jubilo*" by Heinrich Suso, the most popular vernacular writer of the day. He wrote alternate lines in Latin and German.

✧ The earliest English compilation we have is 1426's *Caroles of Cristemas* by Shropshire priest John Audelay. Christian music was gradually shifting from being owned by monks, to being written by monks for popular use. The carols were localized and unique, so the people felt greater ownership of them. In those days you could walk into your pub, sing a local carol, and everyone would join in, rather than nudge each other and start filming you for YouTube.

SENT TO COVENTRY

Medieval Christianity saw reverence grow towards Mary. This shifted attention from Easter towards Christmas, and helped carols transform from uncouth dances to gentler sacred songs, even lullabies. They had a perfect home alongside, or in, the new non-Latin mystery plays. The power of the word was being taken over by the people.

One of our earliest carols still sung, "The Coventry Carol", was taken from the Coventry mystery play, *The Pageant of the Shearmen and Tailors*. The retelling of Herod's Massacre of the Innocents features this brutally sad song – a mother's lullaby to her doomed son. It still haunts today, when sung alongside its later, more joyful carolling counterparts:

> *This poor youngling*
> *For whom we do sing*
> *By, by, lully lullay*
> *Lully, lulla, thou little tiny child*
> *By, by, lully lullay.*

Carols became a fine compromise in the push-pull between sacred and secular. Somewhere between the church's Latin chants and the palace's bawdy feasting, carols were the perfect meeting-place. Religious yet popular, earthy yet holy, unique yet united in aim – they safeguarded the future of Christmas.

St Francis' passion for the poor, for performance, and for the prospering of the Christmas message meant a quiet festive takeover. Under Puritan rule in the seventeenth century, the carol would temporarily become little more than poetry for individual contemplation, still read, rarely sung. For now though, the carol enjoyed centuries as communal celebration, while other Christmas customs were growing too.

Five Christmas trees come early...

✧ *AUSTRIANS...* were starting to bring trees into homes in the Middle Ages, and the first we know of to bring cherry and hawthorn trees inside, where they'd daub them with fruit and nuts.

✧ *ADAM AND EVE...* had a festival day on 24 December, so Germanic Christians linked the Garden of Eden's Tree of Life with Christmas Eve, tying the tree to the festival firmer than you could tie it to a car roof. There were legends that at the moment of Christ's "midwinter" birth, every tree in the world would spark back to life with shoots of green.

✧ *TALLINN, ESTONIA...* claims the first use of the public Christmas tree in the town square. In 1441 a group of bachelor merchants called the Brotherhood of the Blackheads erected a tree in the centre of town, danced around it, then set it on fire, as you would with a Yule log. This trend spread (though the fire didn't), with similar reports from Riga in 1510.

✧ *FRANCE...* was known to have decorated trees in 1521: "They set up fir trees in the parlours of Strasbourg and hang thereon roses cut out of many-coloured paper, apples, wafers, gold foil and sweets." The wafers symbolized the Eucharist; their descendants are the gingerbread men or biscuits hung on trees today.

✧ *MARTIN LUTHER...* didn't just spark the Reformation; a legend tells how he developed Christmas tree decoration. Admiring the forest and the night sky, he was enthralled by a starlit fir tree and recalled the star over Bethlehem. He tried to convey this scene to his family, but words failed him, so he felled the tree and brought it home, adding candles to recreate the starry night. His wife presumably then said, "You could have just told us, Martin." This was thought to be the first traditional German Christmas tree: the *Christbaum*.

DECK THE HALLS!

The Germanic trees gained new decorations over the years. The apples and nuts found new friends joined them on the branches: gingerbreads, sweets, even sweetmeats (you've never hung meat on a tree? You haven't lived). There were coloured paper decorations – although with candles a few inches away, the colour of this paper often went through yellow, orange, red, then into black dust very quickly. Pricier accoutrements, like glass beads on a string, bear a resemblance to today's wired Christmas lights – and at least if one blew, you didn't have to change the lot.

In Nuremberg in 1610, a new Christmas decoration was unveiled: tinsel. Shredded strips of beaten "fool's gold" silver were draped around wealthy homes, though it was very expensive and far heavier than our modern equivalents. Other materials appeared over the years between the silver and our present-day PVC, though unfortunately they too were rather flammable next to the candles. Countless trees and indeed homes have been lost over the years to the combination of candle and ill-advised decoration. The ancient Scandinavians would think we'd taken their fire tributes a little far.

TOP OF THE TREE

By the sixteenth century, the tops of German trees featured not angels or fairies, but a model of Jesus. Wax figurines made popular presents back in Roman Saturnalia days, and the same material was used here to make moulds of cherubs as well as the infant saviour himself.

However, thanks to reformers like Luther, not content with giving us illuminated tree decorations, the days of idols and icons were numbered. In post-Reformation years, a larger effigy – "the tin-gold angel" – replaced the baby Jesus on top of the tree. It was still intended to represent Jesus, only now with angelic wings – so he's incognito.

Following the Reformation, Christmas would undergo the same transformation as the rest of Western Christianity, and Christmas would once again have to fight for its survival. Crib scenes and carvings of Jesus were seen as idolatrous; they went out of fashion and out of sight.

The Reformation paved the way for the Puritanism of the seventeenth century – and here Christmas had finally met its match.

**A Puritan Governor interrupts Christmas sporting
activities amongst early American settlers, c. 1650**

Chapter 6

Cancel Christmas

(1517–1800)

This chapter covers Christmas' darkest hour – a time of no Nowell. No spoilers about whether it came back or not, but we'll also see how it picked up the pieces – from post-Puritan pantomime to plum pudding.

If you think the "Reformed" church was something to do with turkey ham, or that "Puritan" sounds like a no-frills tanning salon, it's worth remembering that the Protestant Reformation had some knock-on effects for our Christmas.

Sixteen Christmas-changing Reformation-type moments...

✧ 1517… On Halloween, reformer and alleged Christmas tree co-inventor Martin Luther nails what's wrong with the church to the door of the Castle Church in Wittenberg. To paraphrase Dolly Parton, he's writing nine-ty-five (theses). Luther permits celebration of Christmas; other reformers disagree.

✧ 1521… In Wittenberg, Protestant reformer Andreas von Carlstadt performs Christmas Mass in German rather than Latin, probably lasting considerably longer due to the length of the words.

✧ 1522… Luther translates the New Testament into German, so that people can check the reformers' complaints against the papacy. As long as they read German.

✧ 1526… William Tyndale translates the New Testament into English, although it's illegal for fifteen years. It's just in English and German to begin with; Cockney and Klingon translations come significantly later (though are now available).

✧ 1534… Henry VIII does some top-down reforming with his Act of Supremacy. The Church of England pings into life; Henry hears wedding bells, again, and it's not tinnitus.

✧ 1536… The monasteries are dissolved, changing the face of English religion. Unemployment rises by 2%, with thousands of monks, friars, and nuns suddenly out of work. And yes, sorry – a lot of canons were fired (no really, it was very serious at the time).

✧ 1541… The mock role "the Boy Bishop" is one of the first Christmas traditions to be stopped by the Reformation. Spoilsports.

✧ 1559… John Calvin publishes his "Institutes", picking up Luther's mantle and running with it (not too far because the mantle was nailed to the church door. This is all very metaphorical, by the way). Unlike Luther, Calvin does have a problem with Christmas, because it's not biblically sanctioned. He doesn't quite outlaw it; he grumbles to one minister to follow "the moderate course of keeping Christ's birth-day as you are wont to do". Christmas is safe. Ish.

✧ 1560… Scotland goes the extra mile (or 500 miles) – Christmas is banned by the Church of Scotland under John Knox.

✧ 1575… Christmas Day called "Yule Day" in Scotland; punishments handed out to those found playing, dancing, and singing "filthy carols".

✧ 1585… Philip Stubbes' *Anatomie of Abuses* records that, "Especially in Christmas time there is nothing else used but cards, dice, tables, masking, mumming, bowling, and such like footeries… Do they think that they are privileged at that time to do evil?… Be merry in the Lord, but not otherwise, not to swill and gull… The true celebration of the feast of Christmas is, to meditate… upon the incarnation and birth of Jesus Christ, God and man."

✧ 1602… Shakespeare's latest footery – *Twelfth Night, or What You Will* – debuts on, when else, 2 February – not Twelfth Night, but Candlemas. Elizabeth I's habit of requesting Christmas plays often forces Shakespeare to write at very short notice. This was intended to close the Christmas season, though it's not a Christmas play. It's more Roman Saturnalian, full of cross-dressing and mistaken identity.

✧ 1607… King James I of England (where they celebrate Christmas) a.k.a. King James VI of Scotland (where they don't) requests a play for Christmas Day, as well as after-dinner games. The suggestion angers Puritans, Scots, and the king's players who thought they had Christmas off.

✧ 1618… King James reinstates Christmas in Scotland, but hardly anyone turns up to celebrate it.

✧ 1640… Scotland bans Christmas again.

✧ 1958… Scotland officially reinstates Christmas after a three-century break. In the meantime a New Year celebration, Hogmanay, has filled the gap.

The religious landscape was changing dramatically, and not just in the area of dramatics. Christmas itself was undergoing its own identity crisis, trying on a bunch of different masks and seeing if anyone applauded. Should it be forty days long, or twelve, or zero? Was Christmas Day a time for elaborate dining, or for celebrating in church, or, as many in the church thought, for neither?

The battle for Christmas had been under way for some time, according to Steve Roud's book *The English Year* – this was "the culmination of a long and bitter struggle for the soul of the festival". Somewhere between the pagan roots of the festival and the superstitions and iconography of the Catholic Church, the infant Jesus was crying to be heard.

REXIT

The reformers drove a wedge into the European church, causing many churches to split from Rome – the "Rexit" of the day (or as it's The Vatican, "Vexit"?). Ripples were felt through many of our favourite Christmas customs; St Nicholas could calm waves for sailors, but could he weather this storm?

Protestant churches effectively downgraded the role or at least the nature of Mary, from what they saw as borderline idolatry. Their Christmas celebrations focused in on the infant Jesus, rather than those around him. Saints' days were discouraged, sparking an attempted coup on St Nicholas himself. His celebration day of 6 December was no longer a day of gift-giving – but it's not that easy to take the gifts away. So instead they were postponed, to Christmas Eve. The "*Christkindl*", the Christ-child, would be the new bringer of gifts rather than this saint.

Christmas was still celebrated by many of the new denominations, notably amongst Lutherans in the Dutch Reformed Church. They would soon make the jump across the ocean and shape the way the festive season was celebrated in America. The Puritans in England however were about to take a much harder line.

A "HAPPY" PURITAN CHRISTMAS

Puritanism was a new extreme form of Protestantism in mid-seventeenth-century England, and it was on the march. As a wing that shunned Catholicism, including its Mass, a festival named after "Christ's Mass" was bound to be in the firing line. Many observed that the level of ungodly behaviour at Christmas was a sure sign that the festival should be done away with.

It was a slow and steady takeover, but over time it became clear that everyday folks would have to make a decision: take a stand and celebrate Christmas, or see it as a festival of idol worship? Simple acts like singing a carol or hanging evergreens became deliberate acts of defiance.

When the Protestant Scots successfully outlawed Christmas in 1640, the English Puritans found a new zeal. In September 1643, an agreement was signed between English MPs and the Scots: in exchange for military aid from the north, English MPs would ensure further reformation of the Church of England. That Christmas would be the time of reckoning.

On our sixth date of Christmas…
(London, 25 December 1643)

Today is a test: of the mettle of the English people across the land. On previous Christmas Days, shops remained closed and churches opened. On this Christmas Day, we see sporadic occurrences of the opposite. Some London shops open for business in a show of allegiance to the government's cause. Further down the road, the closed church doors baffle some who had intended to worship, although the Puritan sympathies of the minister are well-known. Across London, Parliament is not officially sitting (that will be for a Christmas to come), but Puritan MPs make a point of showing up. For them, Christmas is a day like any other. Until it falls on a Sunday. Like next year. And then it's like any Sunday.

Christmas is still legally celebrated across England, but today is a line in the sand, to propel everyday folk into action. Now that we have English Bibles, the people can read for themselves that Christmas celebration is not biblical. The early church fathers took many years to approve its celebration. Perhaps they were wrong to finally cave?

Today all will choose a side. Against the Puritans, there are traditionalists and royalists, who agree with the satirist John Taylor's mourning words: "Thus are the merry lords of misrule suppressed by the mad lords of bad rule at Westminster." But there are many Puritan sympathizers at ground level, who agree with Parliament's ordinance of just a fortnight ago: "The sins of our forefathers… have turned this feast, pretending the memory of Christ, into an extreme forgetfulness of him, by giving liberty to carnal and sensual delights."

WE WISH YOU A MERRY "PROFANE MAN'S RANTING DAY"...

The twenty-fifth of December 1644 fell on a Sunday, usually a fasting day – so this was a chance for a further test. Feast or fast? Eating a dinner oddly became a political protest. Christmas Day gained nicknames among its opponents: non-conformist minister Hezekiah Woodward later labelled it "The old Heathens' Feasting Day, in honour of Saturn, their Idol-God, the Papists' Massing Day, the Profane Man's Ranting Day, the Superstitious Man's Idol Day, the Multitudes' Idle Day, Satan's Working Day, and the True Christian Man's Fasting Day". His point was not subtle: a true Christian fasts on Christmas Day… and doesn't call it Christmas Day.

Christmas 1645 went one step further: it simply didn't exist. There were those that celebrated it across England, but it was no longer an officially recognized celebration. Parliament continued as usual, although some MPs were seen yawning, kept up all night by loud, brazen carollers.

Christmas 1646 saw protestors both pro- and anti-Christmas, the former coming to blows against the shopkeepers who dared open their shops. The poor especially dissented. They loved this annual break from the norm, plus they were a conservative bunch who enjoyed tradition. Christmas was symbolic of the noble ideals that Cromwell and his cronies were trying to vanquish.

For a while they succeeded: Parliament passed a law in June 1647 banning any celebration of Christmas at all. It was no longer enough to simply ignore it – it would no longer be tolerated. Christmas Day that year became another major test. Who would defy the ban and who would uphold it? Daring defenders of Christmas covertly decorated public places with evergreens at great risk; the Lord Mayor of London rode around the city setting fire to any he saw. Some churches opened their doors for Christmas services, and their ministers were promptly jailed. Rioting broke out across the country, particularly in the east of England. Ipswich saw one protestor known only as "Christmas" killed in the riots: yes, the Puritans had succeeded in killing Christmas itself.

In Canterbury the riots were fierce and lasted weeks, with protesters attacking shops who opened their doors on Christmas morning. Pro-Christmas supporters seized control of the city in what seemed like a last stand to protect the festival.

THE GLASTONBURY THORN

As Cromwell's Roundheads battled Royalist Cavaliers in the English Civil War, traditions became targets, including the legendary Glastonbury Thorn. The story went that Joseph of Arimathea walked here, and where his walking stick touched the ground, this thorn grew and remained through the centuries. Every Christmas the monarch would be sent a sprig, till now. There was no monarch, and soon there would be no sprig – it was destroyed by Roundhead troops in another symbolic annihilation of Christmas and its icons. Cuttings had been taken though, so the descendants of the original tree still prosper today.

FATHER CHRISTMAS: POLITICAL ACTIVIST

To appease the working folk who mourned Christmas, the government allowed the second Tuesday of every month as a day off, making twelve a year, to cover the twelve days of Christmas that used to be enjoyed as a holiday. It wasn't just MPs who were to work on Christmas Day – every workplace was to continue as usual. Humbug to that...

Some flouted the ban – even in Parliament. Their Christmas Day session of 1656 featured business as usual, though it was noted by Colonel Joachim Matthews, Member of Parliament for Maldon, that attendance was sparse. Others in the chamber observed that their commute to Westminster had passed streets with "not a shop open, nor a creature stirring". Not even a mouse, to quote a poet we'll meet a century and a half later.

Attending church became risky business. Armed guards confronted those taking Christmas communion, threatening violence if they took the bread and wine. At Christmas 1657, John Evelyn wrote of muskets aimed at him and his wife as they took communion – the guards didn't fire but did arrest them.

Old Father Christmas himself became a symbol of the old England that must be protected in this time of Christmaslessness. Once again, even when Christmas was outlawed, we see people harking back to a forgotten glorious age of Ye Olde Christmas Celebration. Memories had to be kept alive, and nostalgia was used as a weapon, to galvanize support and encourage a return to yesteryear. Pamphlets contrasted the famed bearded chap, happy, if not yet jolly, with the miserable piety of Puritanism. Father Christmas was now the face of political propaganda.

POLITICAL PIE-EATING

Some familiar Christmas comestibles emerged from the Puritan ashes. The Christmas pie had previously been crammed full of all sorts of food scraps and fashioned into a crib-shape, with a small pastry baby Jesus sometimes placed on top. In the old days it was gluttonous, now it was idolatrous.

Plum pudding was banned too, causing the Plum Pudding riots in 1658, back in that hotbed of unrest, Canterbury. Three thousand armed soldiers were sent to enforce the new culinary law and keep order.

The people of England were enterprising folk though. They would find a way around any ban in order to eat the food they wanted. For some this meant ordering from Europe. For others, the letter of the law seemed to target the shape of pies, so if a crib shape was outlawed, how about something that couldn't be confused for a crib? Rather than rectangular, let's try something round. Oh and we'd better not call it a Christmas pie – that's banned. It's full of mincemeat (well, not necessarily full, but there's bound to be a little sweetmeat inside if we can afford it), so there's a name: the mince pie. Change the shape, change the name, flout the ban.

Christmas pie consumption on 25 December is still officially illegal in England. The government hasn't seen the need to overturn it, because no one's really eating Christmas pies any more. As for mince pies, the average Brit will guzzle twenty-seven of them this Christmas season.

CHRISTMAS IN AMERICA

Christmas returned to old England along with Charles II in 1660. In New England though, a ban was just taking hold. The Pilgrim Fathers had docked to find new ground for their Puritanism, without centuries of Christmas tradition to offer resistance – no Father Christmas pamphlets here.

There were other settlers too though. The first American Christmas was a French one, celebrated off the coast of Maine in 1604. A few years later in Jamestown, Virginia, Captain John Smith had Christmas dinner "among the savages... with plenty of good oysters, fish, flesh, wilde fowl and good bread".

But while Protestants in Virginia and New York enjoyed their Christmases, pilgrims farther up the coast were Puritans and Presbyterians, who saw nothing to celebrate. Christmas was no day of rest, and Boston banned Christmas in 1659.

When the law was repealed two decades later, there was still reluctance to celebrate. English customs were increasingly frowned upon, Christmas included. It took nearly 200 years before many Americans warmed to Christmas again.

Peter Kalm, a Swedish naturalist visiting Philadelphia in 1749, wrote in his diary of the evergreen decorations in the Catholic church he visited, though he observed different customs elsewhere: "The Quakers did not regard this day any more remarkable than other days. Stores were open, and anyone might sell or purchase what he wanted.... There was no more baking of bread for the Christmas festival than for other days; and no Christmas porridge on Christmas Eve!"

UNDERNEATH THE MISTLETOE

In Restoration England, Christmas wasn't thriving upon its return either. Samuel Pepys records falling asleep in a dull sermon. Pro-

Christmas propaganda had painted Christmas as a noble English custom, loved and cherished by our forefathers, but now it was back, it wasn't living up to its rose-tinted promise.

The Christmas break had seen off some customs. One involved an effigy of the holy family being placed above the inside of a home's front door, nestled with holly, ivy, or mistletoe. The local priest would tour the parish and bless the homes, embracing the homeowner at the threshold in a display of Christian love. The embrace became a kiss – just a peck on the cheek, nothing too raunchy – and over time that became a kiss not just by the priest, but by anyone underneath it, by way of a greeting. The effigy was seen off by the Reformation's anti-idolatry stance, so the holy family vanished and evergreens remained. It was called a "kissing bough" – two hoops formed a globe, decorated with fruit and greenery, including mistletoe (because it's weird to just kiss under apples).

Mistletoe's popularity for the sub-plant smooch was down to its berries, easily pluckable (steady) with each kiss. The Christmas smackers were therefore happily finite – too many eager well-wishers (or one persistent one) can prove tiresome. Its origins may seem pagan or bawdy, but mistletoe has grown from that greeting of Christian love.

A TOAST!

One day in the late seventeenth century, two young men visited the famous public baths in England's no-idea-how-it-got-that-name city of Bath. A delightful young lady was reclining there, so one of the young men dipped a cup into the water, and drank to her health. The other wryly quipped that rather than drink that liquor (i.e. bathwater), he'd prefer the toast (i.e. the tasty accompaniment). Since that encounter, a pretty lass became described as "the toast of the town", and raising a glass to her health became "raising a toast". So the next time someone raises a toast to the Queen, consider how far we've come from that woman and two bawdy men in the public baths.

The wassail bowl was still popular in England for drinking to the health of friends at Christmas, even if the mystical significance of the apple tree in the orchard had faded. The wassail bowl became a punchbowl, but the raising of toasts remained, whether or not we drink from the same bowl.

Accompanying the wassailing was Twelfth Cake. It was consumed at Twelfth Night parties, with eating, drinking, and games not far removed from the Roman Kalends festival. Twelfth Cake contained a dried bean or pea, creating a king and queen for the night, like the dinner-party equivalent of the medieval Lord of Misrule. Old customs were finding new ways to stay on at the party.

Three seventeenth-century sweet treats...

✧ *THE CANE CHILDREN LOVE...* In 1670 the choirmaster of Cologne cathedral was planning his usual Nativity plays and found a novel way to keep the distracted children quiet. Giving them something to eat was a fine idea, but bending a stick of sugared candy to resemble a shepherd's crook was his stroke of genius. This would remind them of the shepherds' significance at the Nativity, while also giving them something to gnaw on during the performance. As for the sugar rush that followed, let the parents worry about that later. He handed out several that Christmas, and after stripes were added in the twentieth century, over a billion candy canes now sell each year.

✧ *ROYAL DESSERTS...* Proliferating trade routes meant new and exciting foodstuffs found their way to the royal table – King Charles II was one of the first in Britain to eat a pineapple, and the first in history to put ice cream on a ceremonial menu. He was served on bended knee, with his mouth dabbed between mouthfuls. Table décor was sparse, but the food displays made up for it, from a two-foot high castle-shaped salt cellar to wine-flowing fountains. 1671's dinner boasted 145 dishes in the first course alone.

✧ *PLUM PUDDING…* King George I was German, and new to English shores in 1714. He so enjoyed the plum pudding at his first English Christmas, his new nation nicknamed him "The Plum Pudding King". The dish was very popular; 1714 saw one of its first appearances in Mary Kettilby's recipe book *A Collection of above Three Hundred Receipts in Cookery, Physick and Surgery*, where it sat alongside the first recipe for orange marmalade.

REGIONAL VARIATIONS

By now, Christmas dinner looked not dissimilar to how we have it today: turkey, chicken, beef or goose, lots of root vegetables, mince pies, and plum (or Christmas) pudding galore. Christmas porridge was duelling Christmas pudding for its place on the dinner table, and by 1800 we had our victor: pudding. Christmas porridge is surely due a comeback.

There were local variations. The south favoured mince pies made of sugar, currants, fruit peel, spices, eggs and, yes, actual meat – often cow tongue. The north preferred classic Christmas pie, with a game bird filling.

Ireland especially enjoyed a Boxing Day hunt, though it died out in England in the nineteenth century. Also on the wane were the obligatory gifts to landowners or noblemen based on their rank. Gift-giving was becoming more familial rather than hierarchical, partly thanks to the rise of advertising in pamphlets and periodicals. Common folk were encouraged to buy gifts for loved ones, especially children – the century-long remoulding of Christmas as a children's festival began with the rise of advertising, and we'll see it grow through new children's carols, the Victorian family, and Santa. Christmas was already starting to get commercial. Always starts earlier than you think, doesn't it?

Five superstitions if, like Pope Pius VI in 1717, you were born on Christmas Day...

✧ *YOU'LL HAVE GREAT LUCK...* Christmas-born entrepreneurs Messrs Hilton and Chevrolet certainly did.

✧ *YOU'LL NEVER SEE A GHOST...* Apple-dropping physicist Isaac Newton was born on 25 December, and he never saw a ghost. He was deeply religious, but actively spoke against belief in ghoulies (ghosts probably didn't like him because of all the gravity).

✧ *BORN ON A CHRISTMAS WEDNESDAY?* You'll be brave and joyful... Certainly true of popular Countess Noël Leslie, heroine and impromptu tiller of a Titanic lifeboat. (And yes, statistically more people called "Noël" are born at Christmas. What are the chances?)

✧ *YOU'RE MORE LIKELY TO TURN INTO A WEREWOLF*, apparently... Pogues singer Shane MacGowan has a Christmas birthday. Just saying.

✧ *YOU WON'T BE DROWNED OR HANGED...* Pope Pius VI wasn't, though he did die as a captive of Napoleon, having reigned longer than any pope. Great luck!

A MODERN ENTERTAINMENT? OH NO IT ISN'T...

In terms of good old-fashioned festive entertainment, mummers' plays were still delivering, but merging with international dramatic influences. The twenty-sixth of December 1717 arguably saw the birth of a new theatrical form on the London stage, as mumming fused with the Italian Harlequinade in John Rich's pantomime, *Harlequin Executed* – creating the Great British panto.

Rich had inherited the Lincoln's Inn Fields Theatre from his father, but unfortunately failed to wow with tragic roles, so drifted into comedy (I know the feeling). He took the familiar role of Harlequin – and for the first time shut him up. The silent clown emerged, and the show was a hit. The reason for the silence was actually censorship. For fear of dissent, there was a citywide restriction on spoken drama. While Europe put on similar comic plays, London cultivated a unique mime show of its own.

Favourite characters were imported from the continental *commedia dell'arte*: young lovers, old man Pantaloon, and a collection of servants like Scaramouche and Pierrot. The stories would change, but the staples of modern British pantomimes were there – clowning servants, youthful love, and a grotesque character or two. Opera and ballet joined the clowning for an anarchic hotchpotch of all-round entertainment.

One familiar trope was the "transformation scene": Harlequin would hit the scenery with his magic wand and it would change with much backstage wizardry. This wand was actually the bat from traditional *commedia dell'arte*, known for causing a loud slapping sound without transferring much force – literally a "slap stick". John Rich's intertwining of stagecraft and story, though popular long before him in different forms, paved the way for the wondrous transformations in British pantos today, whether

Cinderella's magical ballgown or a quick set change from Jack's beanstalk to giant's lair.

These new pantomimes were less serious than the mystery plays and more ambitious than the mummers' plays. The Italian elements were very fashionable, anarchic, and popular with crowds. When cross-dressing dames appeared years later, they were a perfect fit for the topsy-turvy Roman-style celebrations of yesteryear, channelling the ancient Lord of Misrule as they directed singalongs from the stage.

These plays were lowbrow yet highly popular, especially thanks to actors like David Garrick and the clown-to-end-all-clowns Joseph Grimaldi. By the 1800s, pantomimes were popular family Christmas outings, with Harlequin's chase scene being the children's favourite.

Vaudeville and music hall influenced them further, and there came a need for fuller storylines. Just as in their Harlequinade roots, people preferred classic tales, so that the audience would follow the story easily, and focus on the fun and games added on top. Traditional fairy tales became a popular choice.

One of the most famous, *Peter Pan*, debuted at Christmas 1904, not as a pantomime but a serious play. The audience of adults were surprised when the curtain rose to discover a play for children, though children who did see it that winter were petrified by Captain Hook (fearsomely portrayed by Sir Gerald du Maurier, father of novelist Daphne). Many fainted and had to be carried out.

Oh yes they did.

FADING AWAY?

Festive distraction aside, Christmas itself was losing the attention of everyday folk by the end of the 1700s. 1752's change from Julian calendar to Gregorian calendar probably didn't help. The third of September suddenly jumped to 14 September in the blink of an eye to readjust the dating system, so doubts grew about exactly what people were celebrating and when.

Christmas had fought against Puritanism and survived, but now the novelty seemed to be wearing off. The "Merrie Old England" of yore, promised in Christmas' darkest day by no less than Father Christmas himself, was proving rather difficult to rediscover.

It would take the Victorian era to relight the seasonal fire, but in the meantime the church had to protect this festival that it had fought for. That meant engaging its Christmas attendees culturally: with the carol.

MRS. ALEXANDER.
(*Photograph by A. Aylon.*)

**Cecil Frances Alexander, author of
Hymns for Little Children, including
"Once in Royal David's City"**

Chapter 7

All is Quiet

(1700–1861)

"All persons say how differently this season was observed in their father's days, and speak of old ceremonies and old festivities as things which are obsolete."

So wrote poet Robert Southey in 1807. By now Christmas was out of fashion. To paraphrase the new London pantomimes being performed at the time: Christmas, your best days are *behind you*. In this chapter, we'll see how a few individuals sparked a quiet revolution in Christmas culture.

THANKS FOR THE EGGNOG

While churches on both sides of the Atlantic couldn't decide whether or not to celebrate Christmas, new celebration days crept in. In Scotland, that meant Hogmanay; in North America, Thanksgiving.

It was celebrated as early as the American Christmas, with new (and hungry) pilgrims grateful for the harvest. Britain had its Harvest Festival, but American Thanksgiving would grow into something far bigger. It took till 1789 to become an official day of celebration under George Washington and then came to mark the start of the holiday season, which now covers the Christian Christmas, the Jewish Hanukkah, and the African American Kwanzaa.

As well as Thanksgiving, George Washington gave us the US Constitution, a new form of threshing barn, and even helped along that classic seasonal beverage, eggnog. Its English ancestor was posset, a fourteenth-century drink whose milk and sherry contents eventually priced it out of the market for most Europeans. In the New World though, milk was easy to come by thanks to the expanse of farmland, and they also thought to add the egg. Booze taxation necessitated a shift to the plentiful Caribbean drink of rum, until the American Revolution made rum trickier and whisky (especially bourbon) an easier substitute.

Captain John Smith gave one of the earliest records of drinking it, around the same time that his life was saved by Pocahontas. Presidents Washington and Eisenhower both published potent recipes of the stuff, with the former spending 7 per cent of his presidential salary on alcohol. There's proof.

WAIT UP

While new festivals broke new ground in the New World, Britain was trying to cling to the past. Carols had returned after the Restoration, along with the practice of singing for alms. "Waits" were street musicians licensed to collect money in the Christmas build-up – the ancestor of today's pre-Christmas busker wearing a Santa hat to up the donations. One favourite, dating back to at least the 1500s, was "God Rest Ye Merry, Gentlemen" (notably the "rest" is what's "merry", not the "gentlemen").

But people weren't singing carols like they used to. Amid fears they might die out, there were eager attempts by enthusiasts to document the carols once sung. At the end of the eighteenth century, a Cornish MP, Davies Gilbert, used his parliamentary position to do what many folklorists could not, and implored the country to send him every carol in living memory for preservation. The result was not vast: his first collection totalled eight tunes. It was down to individual hobbyists and rogue MPs to reclaim the carol. The church wasn't joining in.

It wasn't just that the sheet music wasn't as readily available as today. It was more that each carol had local variations and no set tune. Worshippers might have known up to a dozen different tunes, so rather than teach new ones, new hymns adopted these old melodies. A hymn would be introduced by telling the congregation which tune they'd sing it to today.

Common metre, short metre, and long metre were three typical musical metres; so all songs in common metre would be sung to the same two or three tunes. Common metre was indeed the most common – very useful when encouraging illiterate churchgoers to sing, but less useful when trying to document historical carols, and re-energize a post-Puritan Christmas. William Sandys' 1833 publication *Christmas Carols Old and New* compiled eighty carols, but only eighteen tunes. We haven't given up on common metre today – I can report from when I've toured Christmas shows around venues, from theatres to churches, that fun can be had singing "Amazing Grace" to the tune of "Pop Goes the Weasel" or the *Benny Hill* theme.

"While Shepherds Watched Their Flocks" is a good example. Again it's in common metre, and mostly sung to either the tune "Winchester Old" or a variation of a Handel aria (or try "House of the Rising Sun" or "Supercalifragilisticexpialidocious").

THE ONLY LEGAL CAROL

"While Shepherds Watched Their Flocks" reigned supreme for a century as the only Christmas hymn authorized by the Church of England in the 1700s. The Anglican church was very careful about which hymns were biblically accurate enough to be permitted in sung worship. "I Saw Three Ships", for example, dating back to at least the 1600s, didn't stand up to a literal interpretation: how can anyone see three ships sailing into Bethlehem, when it's twenty miles inland? William Sandys preserved it in his collection, but it remained unsung by a cautious church for some time.

"While Shepherds" passed the test, with biblical accuracy throughout, and no origins in secular folk songs. Its author was Poet Laureate, with an Irish Puritan father who'd dedicate sermons to Cromwell (I've never heard anyone dedicate a sermon to anyone – "This one goes out to Ollie Crommers…" just doesn't sit right). With such a perfect résumé, the carol was distributed nationwide in 1700 with the Book of Common Prayer with fifteen non-Christmas-related songs. Three centuries later, it's the only song from that supplement still sung today.

This was one of the carols successfully curated by Davies Gilbert MP, who died on, of all days, Christmas Eve at the age of 72, the sound of carollers hopefully not far from his door.

Six eighteenth-century musical masterpieces…

✧ *WATTS' "JOY TO THE WORLD"*… This 1719 rewrite of a psalm sounds Christmassy now, but it was written about Christ's return at the end of days, not the Bethlehem birth. Music probably by Handel, the first eight notes are actually a simple scale backwards. We all could have written that.

✧ *BACH'S* CHRISTMAS ORATORIO… An early classical Christmas offering, conducted by its composer in Leipzig in 1734. Baroque 'n' roll.

✧ *WESLEY'S "HARK! HOW ALL THE WELKIN RINGS"*… Er, don't you mean "Hark! The Herald Angels Sing"? Well yes, Methodist leader Charles Wesley wrote the original in 1739 on hearing chiming Christmas church bells. It was first sung to the same tune as the hymn "Christ the Lord is Risen Today"; today's familiar tune was written a century later by Queen Victoria's favourite notesmith, Felix Mendelssohn. He wrote this music for the four-hundredth anniversary of the printing press, and expressly requested that the "soldier-like and buxom" tune should never be used for religious purposes. Then he died, and, well… whoops.

✧ *HANDEL'S* MESSIAH… The Christmas classic was written for Easter, in Handel's hour of debt and depression in 1741. He was in London writing Italian opera, but his audience were preferring English-language fare (thanks St Francis of Assisi, see what you've started with your vernacular chants?). Friend Charles Jennens asked Handel to compose something for a libretto he'd written – a last-ditch attempt to keep him in London. The epic piece, "Hallelujah Chorus" and all, was written in twenty-four days, in which time Handel "did think I did see all Heaven before me and the great God himself". It debuted in Dublin in April 1742, just in time for Easter (nearer Jesus' real birthday anyway).

✧ *JOHN BYROM'S "CHRISTIANS AWAKE!"*… was a Christmas gift poem for his daughter, before music was added. Byrom also created a modern shorthand writing system – though that would be an even weirder present than a poem.

✧ *"THE TWELVE DAYS OF CHRISTMAS"*… was sung from around 1780, probably as a French children's memory game, with forfeits for whoever couldn't remember all of the items. The church seemingly retrofitted different facets of the faith to the numbers – the two turtle-doves were the Old and New Testament, the three French hens were faith, hope, and love, and so on. Either way, there was no tune but a chant; our music was added in 1909 by Englishman Frederic Austin, who dragged out the "five gold rings".

CHRISTINGLE OR KRIS KRINGLE?

Two small Germanic churches gave quiet welcomes to two particular Christmas customs around this time. In the first, Moravian minister John de Watteville came up with a new visual aid on 20 December 1747, at a children's service in Marienborn, Germany. To help explain Jesus, he lit candles for each child and tied them with red ribbon – to signify the Light of the World and the blood shed for humanity. He concluded with a prayer: "Lord Jesus, kindle a flame in these children's hearts, that theirs like Thine become."

In 1968, John Pensom of the Children's Society revived and updated the service. To raise funds, children would donate money and receive an orange in return. Now the orange represents the world, the ribbon wrapped around it in love, while four cocktail sticks – with fruit, nuts, marshmallows, and Jelly Tots – represent the four seasons and fruits of the earth.

The name "Christingle" means "Christ fire" – not to be confused with "Kris Kringle", which is either an old name for Santa Claus, the name of Richard Attenborough's character in *Miracle on 34th Street*, or another name for "Secret Santa" in some parts of the world.

Seventy years after de Watteville, inspiration struck another small-town priest, in the alpine settlement of Oberndorf. A broken church organ was the catalyst for what would become the world's favourite carol.

On our seventh date of Christmas...
(Austria, 24 December 1818)
Oberndorf is dwarfed by its neighbour, the grand city of Salzburg, birthplace of Mozart sixty years earlier. But on this

Christmas Eve, the smaller town will host the creation of a musical piece to outperform even Wolfgang himself.

Walking a chilly two miles to his friend's house is assistant priest to the local Catholic church, Father Joseph Mohr. His beginnings were humble – after his illegitimate birth he was named after his godfather, Salzburg's final official executioner. Unwelcome in many occupations, Joseph found his calling at a Benedictine monastery where he showed a flair for music. He wrote poetry and played violin and guitar throughout his priesthood, and two years ago penned the words he carries today: a poem called "Stille Nacht".

At the house of church organist and schoolmaster Franz Gruber, Joseph explains the urgency of their problem: it's Christmas Eve, Midnight Mass tonight, and the organ has been damaged by mice (they should never have been playing it). It's a small church and they can cope without – but on Christmas Eve? Some inspirational music is needed.

Father Joseph shows Gruber his six-verse poem and asks him to work his creative magic. A few hours later, Gruber finishes the melody in time for the two friends to learn it. That night, the simple arrangement for two voices and a guitar greatly moves the small congregation. One day, the song will become the most performed in all of history.

Starting at the aptly Christmas-named St Nicholas' church, the song spread locally at first, till an organ repairer heard the story, and the song, and took the sheet music with him as he travelled. Today "Silent Night" has been translated into 140 languages, and has been designated an intangible cultural heritage by UNESCO.

CAROLS COME OF AGE

Carols steadily returned to Christmas; many like "Silent Night" were poems set to music much later. One 1848 publication of poems was especially significant. *Hymns for Little Children* explained Christianity simply and effectively, with Irish poet Cecil Frances Alexander answering children's questions in verse – and inadvertently creating three world-famous hymns. When asked who made the world, she presented "All Things Bright and Beautiful". A few pages on, there's an answer to questions of life after death: "There is a Green Hill Far Away". On questions of Jesus' birth, she gave her poem "Once in Royal David's City".

The book was an instant hit, and the music only came later. Their author turned down requests to write more, instead dedicating herself to working with the sick and poor. Proceeds from her bestseller went to build the Derry and Raphoe Diocesan Institution for the Deaf and Dumb.

The new carols didn't necessarily focus just on children, as we see in Reverend Dr John Mason Neale's "O Come, O Come Emmanuel" and "Good King Wenceslas", written within five years of Alexander's publication. New carols and customs were arriving thick and fast.

Two decades later, "O Little Town of Bethlehem" was written after a visit to the Holy Land. Influential compilations like 1861's *Hymns Ancient and Modern* ushered such carols into the church, helped by the shift from gallery singers to new church organs. Newer denominations had sung worship at the heart of their services, such as Methodism's sung devotionals. It all led to a choral renaissance in church.

Some of these carols helped put children at the centre of Christmas like never before. If not the church as an institution, then individual Christian creative writers took the chance to

zoom in on the crib. Eighteenth-century festive music, from "Hallelujahs" to "Herald Angels", had focused on the Nativity's heavenly aspects. In the nineteenth century, attention shifted to Jesus the human infant, and Christmas' new lower target age has endured ever since.

JINGLE ALL THE WAY INTO SPACE...

Even a song like "Jingle Bells", now thought of as secular, was written for a Sunday School. Its 1857 Boston debut was at Thanksgiving though, and was more about keeping the children happy. In December 1965, it became the first song broadcast from space – and part of the first astronautical prank. From *Gemini 6*, Wally Schirra and Thomas P. Stafford told Mission Control, "We have an object, looks like a satellite going from north to south, probably in polar orbit... I see a command module and eight smaller modules in front. The pilot of the command module is wearing a red suit..." Then they broke into song, with a harmonica and sleigh bells they'd somehow smuggled on board.

Back in 1857, another song started life as a Christmas gift: Dr John Hopkins wrote "We Three Kings" for his nephews and nieces. There were a lot of writers scrimping on Christmas presents – and he wasn't the first Christian academic to give a festive poem to his young relatives. A few decades earlier, one such poem hugely altered both the sacred and the secular worlds of Christmas. Oh yes. It's that time, folks. Santa Claus was coming to town.

**Merry Old Santa holding toys and pipe with
holly in his cap, by Thomas Nast, published in
Harper's Weekly 1881**

Chapter 8

The Night Before

(1809–1931)

A merica's early settlers may have been Puritans, but others soon followed, and with the Dutch came their own flavour of seasonal celebrations. To hub cities like New Amsterdam (before it became New York), they imported their favourite customs and traditions, including St Nicholas. The first church planted by Dutch settlers in America was in fact named The Church of Sinterklaas. In this chapter, we'll explore how the legend went global, and became the Santa that we know today.

St Nick survived Protestantism's attack on saints' days, with 6 December remaining a popular celebration in Dutch quarters. The British and Irish settled in pockets along the US east coast, and this only firmed up Dutch tradition. Different nations living side by side made their past more important – and gave them an excuse to party. The more the Irish immigrants enjoyed St Patrick's Day, the more their Dutch neighbours turned the volume up on St Nicholas' Day.

In December 1773 amid the American Revolution, anti-British sentiment reached boiling point with the Boston Tea Party, a chest-sinking rebellion against taxation without representation. That same month, for the first time in print, St Nicholas was nicknamed "St A Claus" by the *New York Gazette*. The imperialist St George fell out of favour along with his namesake the British king, so the Dutch-adopted St Nicholas flew higher and higher. Thus Sinterklaas jumped the pond, while the English Father Christmas effectively sank with the tea.

Around the turn of the nineteenth century, the New York Historical Society chose St Nicholas as their patron saint. The Dutch practice of gift-giving increasingly appealed, especially in a season marked by drinking and violence rather than spiritual, or certainly not family, celebrations. It would take a writer to absorb such local customs and make them national – even international.

KNICKERBOCKER'S GLORY

Washington Irving was an observational satirist, who saw different nationalities coexisting, struggling for a sense of their own past in this still relatively New World. So he wrote satires like his 1809 *History of New York from the Beginning of the World to the End of the Dutch Dynasty*. It wasn't intended to be serious, and he even penned it under a Dutch-sounding pseudonym: Diedrich Knickerbocker (the surname meaning "baker of toy marbles" – that "knick" sound mimics colliding marbles). To sell copies, Irving started one of the first viral marketing campaigns by advertising Knickerbocker as a missing person around New York.

New Yorkers took the book to their hearts, and to this day the great name of Knickerbocker is synonymous with New York. The New York Knicks is the basketball team, while the Knickerbocker Glory is a favourite dessert. Irving's illustrator brought the work to Britain, and women's "knickers" found their name based on pictures of what were originally men's pantaloons. Irving's other contributions included giving notes for Edger Allen Poe's *The Fall of the House of Usher*, and helping spread the fictitious notion that Europeans thought the world was flat. His later works included famous over-sleeper *Rip Van Winkle* (1818) and famous don't-you-dare-sleeper *The Legend of Sleepy Hollow* (1820).

But before all this came that 1809 spoof New York history book, which included frequent mention of the good St Nicholas, now known to some locals as "Sancte Claus". Irving was a member of the New York Historical Society, whose founder John Pintard had for years championed St Nick as New York's rightful patron saint. Irving, fast becoming the world's first internationally best-selling author, popularized this notion of St Nick as New York's finest, while ribbing the Dutch for their devotion towards him.

Irving's version of St Nicholas "came riding over the tops of the trees, in that self-same wagon wherein he brings his yearly presents to children". He veers away from the gaunt bishop of the myths and makes him more accessible – after all, it was a pastiche. He ramped up the Dutch stereotype, modelling him on the sailors at New York's docks, with thick green coat, knee-breeches, and broad-brimmed hat. He'd carry a pipe and a little extra – shall we say – "holiday weight".

The figure of Sinter/Sancte/Santa Claus took hold in American folklore. Many called him "Santy Claus" – easier for children, who were swiftly becoming the character's demographic. The 1821 book *A New-Year's Present, to the Little Ones from Five to Twelve* included reference to "Old Santeclaus", for the first time pulled by a single reindeer. Accompanying illustrations show his wagon packed with gifts for the good, but the closing image has a stocking filled with birch rods to punish the bad. With Norse reindeer and Dutch gift-giving, Mr Claus was drawing together many cultures, like America itself. But he still wasn't fully linked with Christmas.

One year later, in Knickerbocker's own city of New York, another poem brought together more traditions, and sprinkled on a few of its own. Santa shifted from flying Dutch sailor to something more wondrous, a twinkle in his eye. The author was Dr Clement Clarke Moore, an academic far prouder of his work on Hebrew linguistics. This poem was just a bit of fluff for his family, who comprised its first audience on Christmas Eve 1822. Moore had penned it only a day earlier, on Christmas Eve Eve…

On our eighth date of Christmas…
(New York, 23 December 1822)

> 'Twas the night before the night before Christmas, and all through the den,
> Not a sound could be heard, but for Dr Moore's pen.

This man was a minister, preacher, and writer
Who'd penned Hebrew lexicons; now, something lighter.

He'd studied the myths of St Nick worth preserving,
And borrowed ideas from pal Washington Irving.
Till now, the tales told of a wagon, not sleigh,
Flying sixth of December, or perhaps Christmas Day.

So Dr Moore scribbled on Christmas Eve Eve
This tale of St Nick, new notions conceived:
The "jolly old elf" now had "little round belly
That shook, when he laughed, like a bowl full of jelly."

He'd gained extra reindeer: Dasher and Vixen,
Prancer and Dancer, Dunder and Blixem,
Comet and Cupid… And if someone's excluded,
It's a hundred and seventeen years till there's Rudolph.

The chimney – not door – is his favourite entrance,
The easiest route to deliver the presents.
And events shifted earlier, just by one day,
It's now Christmas Eve that he rides on his sleigh.

(For many in church, they saw Christmas as Catholic,
And Dr Moore thought, well this dating's elastic:
Make it the twenty-fourth, don't get embroiled
In questions of spiritual rites getting spoiled.)

The very next day 'twas the night before Christmas,
And Dr Moore debuted "A Visit from St Nicholas".
His children sat listening, a tale before bed,
Enthralled by the words that their father now said:

"'Twas the night before Christmas, when all thro' the house
Not a creature was stirring, not even a mouse…"

AFTER THE NIGHT BEFORE

His children nestled all snug in their beds, Dr Moore would have had no idea that he had just created a modern literary wonder of the world. The following Christmas, a family friend sent the poem to the *Troy Sentinel* newspaper for anonymous publication, and America began to fall for its charms. It would take some years before Moore publicly claimed ownership, preferring anonymity – until others claimed to have written it instead. Soon it became a nationwide family tradition to read it aloud every Christmas Eve.

Moore's new elements shaped the way Americans viewed St Nicholas. Reindeer had been part of the story for a while; the Lapp legend had Old Winter being led by reindeer and as he drove the reindeer south, they'd bring snow. This had a real-world reflection, though the reindeer were escaping the cold, rather than dragging it behind them. These associations had always been with winter, or the man "Winter", rather than Christmas, or this man who brought Christmas, or dragged it behind him.

The end of "A Visit from St Nicholas" gives us the jolly greeting: "Happy Christmas to all, and to all a good-night!" Some later editions tweaked this from "Happy" to "Merry", but at the time of Dr Moore's writing, the only "merry" thing was Merrie Old England, or the drunken hiccupping from too much eggnog. For a "Merry Christmas", we need to wait just a couple of decades for greetings cards – all part of the industry that Dr Moore helped create.

STOCKING TRADE

"Stockings were hung by the chimney with care" all over the country by now, based on St Nicholas' original window-based generosity. As Moore's poem spread, the stocking became an essential part of the growing Christmas industry. Rather than pre-owned socks, stockings would now be made by the family, then as demand grew, bought in markets. Next time we wrap a present (that we've bought) in paper (that we've bought) and place it in a stocking (that we've bought), notice how far we've come from putting an orange into an old sock.

Ten Santa's little helpers – and the gifts they bring...

✧ *ST NICHOLAS OF MYRA...* The man, the legend, the original secret Santa. Brought us undercover gift-giving and stockings by the fireplace.

✧ *THOMAS NABBES OF WORCESTERSHIRE...* The dramatist. In 1638, brought us pictures of an old man in fur and nightcap: Father Christmas. Wait, that's not Santa Claus... is it?

✧ *WASHINGTON IRVING OF NEW YORK...* The bestseller. Brought together Dutch legends and sold it back wholesale as Santa Claus.

✧ *CLEMENT CLARKE MOORE OF NEW YORK...* The Hebrew lexicographer. Packaged it all up in a fun-sized portion with added reindeer and new chimney-based gift delivery options.

- ❖ *T.C. BOYD OF NEW YORK…* The wood engraver. The first to illustrate Clement Clarke Moore's poem, bringing us a jolly, dumpy chap in Dutch breeches and fur hat. Other early American Santas included the jester look: tricorn hat, yellow stockings, and red waistcoat.

- ❖ *THOMAS NAST OF BAVARIA…* The political cartoonist, who also helped popularize Uncle Sam. Brought us hundreds of illustrations to accompany Dr Moore's poem, including a shorter Santa with a cap, sometimes in red. His first Santa had an American flag draped over him, and Lincoln commissioned him to draw Santa visiting both sides of the Civil War. Nast's early drawings weren't too child-friendly; his Bavarian past meant a sterner St Nick and fearsome assistants like Knecht Ruprecht and the Belsnickel. It took years before the pictures softened, becoming less elfin and more human. Nast eventually added Santa's workshop, a home address in the North Pole, and a list.

- ❖ *VIRGINIA O'HANLON OF NEW YORK…* The letter-writer. In 1897 the eight-year-old wrote not to Santa but to *The New York Sun*. After her classmates denied Santa, she asked the paper to rule on his existence. The paper's veteran editor published a long reply, assuring Virginia that her friends were sceptics in a sceptical age: "He exists as certainly as love and generosity and devotion exist… Not believe in Santa Claus! You might as well not believe in fairies…"

- ❖ *L. FRANK BAUM OF CHITTENANGO…* The wizard. His 1902 novel *The Life and Adventures of Santa Claus* gave him ten reindeer, an earned immortality, and a home in the land of Hohaho – though these never caught on. Santa even cropped up in a crossover Oz novel, long before the 1939 film of *The Wizard of Oz* became a Christmas favourite, without a Santa cameo.

✧ *WHITE ROCK BEVERAGES* of, erm, White Rock… The water people. Before Santa found some cola or other, he drank mineral water and ginger ale in White Rock's 1915 campaign, wearing red and white.

✧ *HADDON SUNDBLOM OF FINLAND/SWEDEN/ MICHIGAN…* The corporate illustrator. As well as bringing us the Quaker Oats guy on my porridge packet, from 1931 Sunny gave us the familiar pictures of a black belt, black boots, white fur – and brought The Coca-Cola Company millions in revenue. Oh, and now he's definitely red, and Santa's pipe is replaced by a can of… is it Lilt?

THE CHURCH VS SANTA CLAUS

Perhaps surprisingly, many of Santa's co-creators were Christians. The original St Nicholas was a bishop. Washington Irving served as a vestryman in Christ Episcopal Church in Tarrytown, New York. Dr Clement Clarke Moore was a church planter and Professor of Biblical Learning. Cartoonist Thomas Nast was a staunchly anti-Catholic Protestant, perhaps eager to caricature the world's most famous saint. Of course, Santa also had a Norse god phase (don't we all?).

Perhaps by the mid-nineteenth century, Christianity had made its peace with St Nick's transformation. If you're going to have a caricatured Greek/Norse/Dutch pagan celebrated the world over, he might as well be a noble Christian saint with generosity at his core. Surely that's better than the alternatives?

The innovators were street-level faithful creatives, and top brass disagreed. In 1969, Pope Paul VI downgraded the status of St Nicholas' sainthood, casting doubt on the bishop's origins. But by that point, Santa was off and flying. To reach that point though, like all American imports, he needed a certain Americanisation. Sorry, Americanization. Spellings change too.

SINTERKLAAS VS SANTA CLAUS

St Nick was no exception to the New World's re-ownership process. In his Dutch guise as Sinterklaas, he rewarded good children who knew their prayers, and those who didn't might receive a beating from his cane. It was more of a threat than a practice (it's tricky to be caned by a mythological figure or a deceased saint), but American Santa needed to be nice to all to become a family Christmas icon. So forget the cane-based prayer exams. Instead he'll just have a list and check it twice – probably twice to give the naughty kids a second chance at presents.

Sinterklaas was still yet to be fully Christmas-ised (sorry, Christmas-ized – I'm English, that's why I keep apologizing). The day of gift-giving would somehow drift from 6 December to the 25th, but culture doesn't budge easily – slowly slowly catchy Santa. St Nicholas' Day stayed where (or when) it was, but the new custom had children write their letters on that day, allowing Santa enough time to source their presents for the 25th, when they'd receive them.

SANTA CLAUS VS FATHER CHRISTMAS

American entrepreneurship has always been world-class, so it's no surprise that they succeeded in selling Santa back to the continent he'd come from. Although the Netherlands have been less keen; in recent times, one visiting Santa Claus was chased out of town.

The Finns were early adopters, jumping on the chance to claim Finnish Lapland as Santa's home (and you must come and visit). Other Arctic nations joined in – Canada claims his address has their postcode H0H 0H0, while their Minister of Citizenship, Immigration and Multiculturalism officially stated that "as a Canadian citizen, he has the automatic right to re-enter Canada once his trip around the world is complete" – useful information in a post-Trump world.

Santa's debut in Britain dates back to May 1861, when a racehorse named Santa Claus ran at Epsom. So began the business merger of Santa Claus and Father Christmas – or perhaps a hostile takeover.

Traditionalists in Britain clung to Father Christmas (they still do), and originally there were key differences. Santa brings presents; Father Christmas just brings winter. The American version is child-friendly; the English version less so. Mr Claus wears a two-part suit and hat with white bobble; Mr Christmas wears a long one-piece habit with a hood. To this day the only major difference in appearance is in the subtlety of their headwear – hat versus hood is a handy way to spot an American Santa from an English Father Christmas.

Eight Santa equivalents...

✧ China's Santa is called Dun Che Lao Ren: the Christmas Old Man.

✧ Japan has a Buddhist monk named Hotei-osho, with eyes in the back of his head to keep an eye on children.

✧ Italy has Befana, an old woman riding a broomstick on 5 January. She gives gifts to the good, coals to the not-so-good. Apparently she ignored the Magi as they passed through Italy (ignore the geography), so was cursed to forever seek out the face of the Christ-child among children the world over once a year.

✧ Germany used to have the Christ-child himself – the Christkindl – or perhaps an angel, riding on a deer laden with toys and sweets.

✧ Russia has a female St Nick equivalent – a white-robed elf maiden on a sleigh, with carols sung in her honour.

✧ In Ukraine, it's Father Frost and the Snowflake Girl.

✧ Hawaii has Kanakaloka (if it sounds like "can o' Coca-Cola", that's a coincidence. A Coca-coincidence).

✧ The Moon has Santa Clanger and his whistling mice elves. Alright maybe they don't, but you can't prove otherwise.

SELLING SANTA

By the 1890s, almost every American town had at least a couple of Clauses pop up locally to hand out presents. They were clearly breeding. With this proliferation of Clauses, there was no stopping him. To this day in some American cities, you're never more than five feet away from a Santa Claus. Or that could be rats.

From Moore's elf, via Nast's gnome, to Sundblom's chubby laugher telling us that holidays are indeed coming on December billboards today, he's survived a good few makeovers. St Nicholas the bishop vanished, so his mitre went too. Nicholas the Norse-like god flew off, so his holly crown fell away. He used to hold a crook or pipe, but after discovering the fizzy stuff, he dropped those props and never picked them up again. Sometimes he used to drink wine – not any more, though the rosy cheeks have stayed (red is very helpful for Coke).

But no, mythbusting fans, Coke didn't turn him red – he'd been red before, and green, and black and white… but you could say Coke kept him red, and sold him all over the world. In World War II he'd remind troops of home – and of course they'd leave traces of his customs wherever they'd been.

While America was growing its Santa Claus, England had the whole festival to bring back into fashion. And once again it's partly thanks to Washington Irving for bringing it back to us.

The first Christmas card, designed by John Calcott Horsley
and commissioned by Sir Henry Cole in 1843

Chapter 9

God Bless Us, Every One

(1827–1901)

Hark!

By now we've welcomed many guest traditions to our Christmas party: Santa, carols, tinsel, mince pies, Christmas pud, and there's even a crib scene with a baby Jesus in it somewhere around here. The mistletoe's up and we're trying to fit a Christmas tree through the front door. In fact it's getting a bit packed already. Surely every guest has arrived?

Far from it. The Victorian era brought a pace of advancement at such an alarming rate, blink and you'll miss it. Across Victoria's reign, new guests range from the fairy on the tree to the turkey dinner, from Nine Lessons & Carols to Boxing Day via the white Christmas. We'll welcome paper decorations, the postal service, electric lights, Santa's grotto, and notions of charity and coming home for Christmas. Songs like "Away in a Manger", "Jingle Bells", and "O Little Town of Bethlehem" join our playlist. The Christmas tree grows from localized German ritual to worldwide phenomenon. In the 1840s alone we'll add the Christmas cracker, "Once in Royal David's City", "O Come, All Ye Faithful", Christmas cards, and Dickens' *A Christmas Carol* – and those last three all appeared within weeks of each other in December 1843. Our festive party is about to get very crowded very quickly.

We start this century with Christmas on the decline but we'll end with Christmas almost as we know it: a snowy child-focused festival of generosity and snugness, with even a spot of commercialized window-shopping creeping in.

For much of this we have to thank the Industrial Revolution, the emergence of the new middle class, and three particular wise men: Charles Dickens, Prince Albert, and our old friend Washington Irving. Irving may have sold the Dutch Santa myth to his fellow Americans, but he also sold the classic English Christmas to, yes, the English.

REIGNITING THE FIRE

After the Puritan pause of Christmas in the mid-seventeenth century, England found it hard to get its festive groove back. Merrie Old England had gone, and taken "Old Christmas" with it. *The Times* newspaper made no reference to Christmas Day between 1790 and Queen Victoria's accession to the throne in 1837. It was almost a day like any other, just as the Puritans had planned.

It was still a time for royal feasts – that never changed. By Victoria's reign though, some hierarchical aspects had settled down, and the trend was now to help oneself. Unfortunately for many guests, each course would be removed the moment the Queen had finished eating hers – and of course she had first dibs every time. In such a vast hall, that inevitably meant that some people never managed to be brought their meal before Her Majesty had moved on. She ate fast too, putting away a seven-course dinner in just half an hour. There was a side table for anyone peckish between courses, and a public gallery where anyone could watch this spectacle, but many of those invited still left rather hungry.

Christmas dinners continued in homes across the country, roast meat filling most stomachs, whatever your level in society. Newspapers of December 1827 report that the poor of the Liverpudlian workhouse were given "their annual treat of roast beef and plum-pudding", typical of impoverished Christmases at the time.

For those a notch up, Christmas dinner could be a financial burden, so many workplaces operated a "Goose Club". Employees paid a few pence each week throughout the year to afford a goose on Christmas Day. At all levels, dining was a little more extravagant at this time of year, even if the goose was small. But away from the dinner table, Christmas was going cold.

CHRISTMAS IN RURAL BIRMINGHAM... AND MEXICO

Washington Irving would have known well of the demise of the English Christmas. He crossed the Atlantic for an English winter and wrote a travelogue for the folks back home, noting that Christmas customs "are daily growing more and more faint". Yet he was entranced by the traditions clinging on, so penned some words to revive interest. As with all of Irving's writings, a sheen of exaggeration is ever-present – he liked to satirize, and he liked to amplify tradition into glowing nostalgia.

Another of his oddly named pseudonyms joined Diedrich Knickerbocker: Geoffrey Crayon. In his *Sketch Book* of 1819, Irving (or Crayon) reported on the joyous celebrations of an English country Christmas. He wrote of presents and feasts, rosy-cheeked schoolboys, and carriage rides to grand mansions in the rural settings of Yorkshire and Birmingham (Britain's second city was clearly not the industrial behemoth that it would become – either that or Irving was completely making it up).

One account, "The Stagecoach", tells of the hospitality of the Bracebridges. This semi-fiction was based on Irving's stay with the family of James Watt – steam engine co-inventor, namesake of the "Watt" unit of measurement, creator of the word "horsepower"… and legendary Christmas party host. The generosity of Watt (via the fictional Bracebridge) was inspirational, with carol-singing and a fine spread on the table. Irving's tale "Christmas Eve" went on to explain the significance of – and goings-on beneath – the mistletoe. Fading traditions were rejuvenated by Irving's writings – and went viral across the Western world.

In North America, one new festive element grew thanks to the first United States Minister to Mexico. Dr Joel Roberts Poinsett visited the city of Taxco in the 1820s, and as a keen botanist was delighted to spy a brilliant red-leafed plant. Dr Poinsett sent cuttings back home, where it became the poinsettia, and a Christmas institution.

Traditions don't start that easily though. Like any plant, traditions need a deep grounding before they take root. In this case, Poinsett heard a sixteenth-century legend of a girl too poor to provide a gift for a Christmas celebration, but eager to pay tribute to Christ at Christmas. An angelic instruction led the girl to place weeds in front of the church altar, where they bloomed into beautiful crimson, symbolic of Jesus' blood. Soon after, the plants were included in Mexican Christmas celebrations, emulated by Dr Poinsett as he sent the plant and legend north to the States.

REVIVAL

Sixteenth-century traditions were proving fertile ground in England too, decades into the Industrial Revolution. From railways to factories, technological advancement had given the early Victorians an elevated view of their place in history. Just as fast-moving tech can make today's world feel like tomorrow's, so too did our nineteenth-century counterparts see themselves as people of the future. History for them was less of a continuous line, more a museum to be appreciated, or plundered.

Medieval and Tudor heydays were particularly harked back to. The Christmas seen off by Puritans was thought to be the festival's golden age, just as we have nostalgic views of Victoriana today. It meant that the concept of an "English Christmas" was something to aspire to recreate. In his book *Christmas: A History*, Mark

Connelly notes the intent to "conserve rather than invent, revive rather than inaugurate".

Almost all Victorian traditions were nothing new, but thanks to technology and entrepreneurship they could be reinvigorated. The Christmas card was a reworking of ancient Christmas letters and mottos. The old Christmas tree was popularized. New carols were written in memory of the old… or because no one had memory of the old.

BRINGING CHRISTMAS HOME

The change to the Victorian way of life was the biggest influence on Christmas. Thanks to industrialization, people were flocking from the country to the city. There were a million Londoners in 1800 and nearly 7 million a century later, making London the world's largest city. City life has benefits in terms of employment, but at the cost of community spirit – including wassailing, orchard blessing, mummers touring the village, the parish priest blessing each family home… the list goes on. In the country, more effort went into decorating the village church; urbanites instead decorated where they lived. Public feasting became private feasting. Christmas moved into the home.

The home itself, rather than the house, was becoming a new phenomenon of its own. While the workhouse was in no way a good place to be, advancements in heating, plumbing, and eventually electrics meant that for many, evening and winter had the potential to be enjoyable like never before. (Just wait until radio and television.) The domestication of Christmas was the festival's biggest leap for a millennium. Now customs didn't belong to the community but to the family.

With the workforce gravitating towards cities, there developed the idea of returning home for the family Christmas. In the past, villagers had but a short walk to see relatives; now hordes of city-dwellers made that seasonal exodus back home, like the holy family for the census. New modes of transportation made this possible: trains, or even the omnibus. As the railways developed, people could move further from their birthplace to find work, meaning that a Christmas family reunion was something to especially anticipate, compared with a stroll over a field to say hello to Mum. To this day, we're still moving – as recently as the 1990s, the average Brit lived five miles from their birthplace; at the time of writing, that's now 100 miles.

Employment, transportation, the middle class, the new postal service, popular royals… all of these combined to give Christmas new verve. One movement in particular gave Christmas new character, and that would be the renewed Victorian interest in the arts.

DO YOU WANT TO BUILD A SNOWMAN?

Charles Dickens was born on a February winter's day in 1812. The Thames froze the year before and again in the winter of 1813 – the last time the tidal section would do so. The river was wider and shallower then, so flowed more slowly and froze more easily. The winter of 1536 was so cold that Henry VIII commuted from Westminster to Greenwich across the Thames via sleigh. Incredible Frost Fairs were held: a full high street with street performers, donkey rides, and even an elephant, all on the river. London's last great Frost Fair was held when Dickens turned two. His earliest memories were of such a winter, England in the grip of some of its snowiest weather for 300 years.

The world climate was so bleak in 1816 that it was known as "The Year Without a Summer" or rather macabrely, "Eighteen Hundred and Froze to Death". It was partly responsible for the creation of New York, as bad crops sent migrants from New England farms in search of better fortune, while the poor weather also uprooted and galvanized the founders of Mormonism. The sunless summer forced a gaggle of English writers to adapt their Italian retreat, accepting Lord Byron's challenge to each write a ghostly tale. Mary Shelley emerged with *Frankenstein*; John William Polidori spawned the genre of vampire fiction with his tale *The Vampyre*.

The perennial winter influenced literature more gradually when it came to the young Dickens. 1816's was just one of eight white Christmases in a row in his first eight years. By contrast, London had only seven official white Christmases in the entire twentieth century. The odds of a white Christmas had fallen after 1752's shift from Julian to Gregorian calendar, as 25 December slid nearer autumn. Luckily for our reading pleasure though, Dickens was born at the very end of the "Little Ice Age", following the "Medieval Warm Period". The intensely cold winters between 1500 and the 1850s are preserved for us in art (mid-sixteenth-century paintings became a lot snowier), including Dickens' masterwork. Thanks to his blizzard of a childhood, snowmen and sledging have become fixed as part of the Christmas backdrop. Christmas *was* snow for Dickens – which means it is for us today, whatever the weather.

Building snowmen had been popular since ancient times. Bob Eckstein's *The History of the Snowman* calls snow "free art" for the Middle Ages, while in higher artistic circles Michelangelo was commissioned to make a snowman in 1494. The earliest recorded drawing of a snowman is from 1380; the earliest photograph is from the 1850s.

The climate may have warmed, but Dickens preserved those frosty winters in his writing. He also warmed the hearts of readers, bringing notions of family and charity to Christmas like never before. One particular story led to him being nicknamed by some, "the man who invented Christmas"...

On our ninth date of Christmas...
(London, 19 December 1843)

As Mr Dickens steps into the London street, he can almost feel the snow beneath him – but not quite, because this year he'll have to imagine it. Sadly the weather has not played snowball with his wintry novella; this is the tenth mildest December on record. Still, the seven-degree day means that the streets are busier, and more are out seeking his book on its day of release. Perhaps as they read they'll hark back to white Christmases of yesteryear – after last year's even warmer winter, those wintry days may be behind us for good.

He cannot help but smile as he hears a boy advertise his wares: that he has stock of Mr Dickens' latest work, A Christmas Carol. *He's well-known but his star has been fading a little – perhaps he spent a little too long touring America. The written works too may not have quite delivered as promised. The recent* Martin Chuzzlewit *left Dickens and his publisher out of pocket after sales failed to match the success of* Oliver Twist.

So Dickens is self-publishing this new book, hoping that a cut of the profits will prove wiser than taking a lump sum. Those printing costs have been high though, so this book needs to sell well to turn a profit. The edition appeals to Charles, ever the perfectionist: the red cloth cover and golden pages reflect the colours of Christmas – far better than the ghastly olive endpapers originally printed. It was only finalized two days ago.

Many are parting with their five shillings for a copy. Profiteering aside, Charles' travelling has given him a new perspective on his career – more cultural commentator than writer-for-pleasure – and this is the first major publication since adopting this new role. He has campaigned against slavery in the United States, and following trips to Cornish tin mines and impoverished industrial Manchester, he has been determined to make a difference. In particular Charles wishes to provoke his middle- and upper-class readers into action by highlighting the social injustices under their noses. After a faltering start turned this passion into a political pamphlet, Dickens has instead opted for a Christmas ghost story, a genre with "twenty thousand times the force… [of] my first idea".

This is not the first time that Dickens has written about Christmas. Aged twenty-three he wrote a short essay encouraging warm hearts, nostalgia, and seasonal optimism, reflecting on the year just gone and the many years before. His feelings towards the festival echo those of Sir Walter Scott – who lamented the loss of old Christmas forty years previously – as well as Washington Irving. Dickens once noted, "I do not go to bed two nights out of seven without taking Washington Irving under my arm upstairs to bed with me."

After that, Dickens wrote in The Pickwick Papers *that Christmas "can win us back to the delusions of our childish days". That book included a template for* A Christmas Carol: *a lonely, miserly churchman sees the error of his ways after mystical goblins show him past and future – a story so good it's worth telling properly.*

Pickwick *also included a description of a perfect Christmas at Dingley Dell, just as the subsidiary characters celebrate in* A Christmas Carol. *Christmas is a family occasion for Dickens, and he's looking forward to the two official days off next week with his four young children, wife Kate, and Kate's sister Georgina who lives with them to support the house. What better time to commune with the family than Christmas, when the children can enjoy a parlour game or be baffled by his latest magic trick? One of Charles' sons will later write that he adored this "really jovial time... my father was always at his best, a splendid host, bright and jolly as a boy and throwing his heart and soul into everything that was going on... And then the dance! There was no stopping him!"*

He passes house after house, where later carollers will doubtless be reviving their tradition of singing for money. Charles smirks: he has a carol of his own. His novella is fully titled A Christmas Carol in Prose, Being a Ghost-Story of Christmas. *He's no composer or lyricist, but was keen to add his voice to the carol renaissance of late, and he's even written "staves" (or stanzas) instead of chapters.*

The tale of Ebenezer Scrooge's transformation from miser to philanthropist is a deliberate morality lesson of warmth amid snow, of hot turkey and family cheer. There are glimpses of a middle-class Christmas with party games like Snap Dragon and Blind Man's Buff, as well as a barely struggling working-class dinner with a roast goose and Christmas pudding. There's even mention of a mulled wine called "Smoking Bishop", made from port, red wine, citrus fruit, sugar, and spice. Dickens enjoyed a glass or bowl of Bishop at the upper-middle-class Christmases of his youth, even as a child; after all, alcoholic punch is a safer bet than drinking water.

The book features nostalgic trips to past Christmases – essential in this fast-moving world of railways and factories – as well as a timely reminder to be truly present at our family festivities. There are, of course, ghosts; perhaps the Christmas ghost story will become a trend. Dickens' Ghost of Christmas Present is based on the Roman god Saturn, figurehead of their Saturnalia festival.

Dickens is fond of pacing these streets. While creating this story, he walked "fifteen or twenty miles many a night when all sober folks had gone to bed". He wrote obsessively, starting just two months ago, and while writing, "I wept and laughed, and wept again." Six weeks later the book was complete, with the last pages finished in early December. Already he is mulling discussions for New Year stage adaptations – several different productions will crop up within the month, with his backing or not.

Charles is recognized by one well-wisher out delivering an envelope via the new "Penny Post" system, established just three years ago. Perhaps one day Charles' books may be delivered by similar means – though surely not for a penny. Dickens wonders if that envelope contains one of the brand new Christmas cards, on sale just a few streets away in Sir Henry Cole's art shop. Time will tell if the enterprising experiment works. By Christmas, Sir Henry will sell 1,000 at a shilling each, while today alone, A Christmas Carol will sell six times as many for five times the price. Selling out in a day, more books will be printed to keep up with Christmas demand.

For now, Charles enjoys his walk through London. Next week he will take his young family through these streets to the toy shop in Holborn, for their annual custom of choosing one present each. Hopefully the book will sell well – Kate has a fifth child on the way. If he were visited by a Ghost of Christmas Future, he could be told that within a few years they'll have ten children.

CHARITY BEGINS

Dickens' trump card was painting Scrooge as the hardest of hearts, showing that even he could become the humanitarian of the book's finale. This ushered in a new charitable connection to Christmas, his contemporaries quick to recognize that this was one of the few books to improve the behaviour of those who read it. Yet the story didn't rant; even in poverty, there was the close family joy at Christmas. George Orwell later wrote of the Cratchit family's resilient smiles: "The wolf is at the door, but he is wagging his tail."

The influence of this short book was immediate. Just a few months later, *The Gentleman's Magazine* attributed a boom in charitable giving to *A Christmas Carol*. One American factory-owner read it on Christmas Eve and closed his factory the next day, instead giving a turkey to each employee. *Vanity Fair* author William Makepeace Thackeray noted that, "A Scotch philosopher, who nationally does not keep Christmas Day, on reading the book, sent out for a turkey, and asked two friends to dinner – and that is a fact." Thackeray died on Christmas Eve, twenty years after the book's publication. When Dickens himself died, so entwined was he with the festive season that a Covent Garden barrow-girl was heard to say: "Dickens dead? Then will Father Christmas die too?"

Charity had been associated with Christmas for many years. In 1667 Samuel Pepys reported in his diary that he "stopped and dropped money at five or six places, which I was the willinger to do, it being Christmas". For many years churches had rattled their boxes and monarchs had rewarded their poorer subjects. A year prior to taking the throne, Victoria was so moved by a visit to a gypsy camp that she urged her mother to send for provisions and blankets. She later established a Christmas tradition of handing out hampers at Windsor Castle, providing a ton of bread and half a ton of plum puddings, as well as plenty of beef, potatoes, and coal.

Dickens was a favourite of Victoria's. Whether inspired by him or not, four years after *A Christmas Carol* she ensured extra funds for Christmas dinners at workhouses across the country. This isn't to say that Dickens melted every heart into an outpouring of love for the poor – there was a pervading sense that the poor deserved their place, an attitude still prevalent today. The workhouses were thought to be too good for some people – and they were not good. After political discussion in the 1870s, some parts of London's impoverished East End even had their welfare assistance withdrawn.

BOXING DAY

Church charitable "boxes" were in decline, lasting just long enough for Boxing Day to become an official public holiday, on 26 December 1871. There's an urban legend that the old boxes gave us the word "TIP" – "To Insure Promptness", but there's no evidence for this. Another misunderstanding is that Boxing Day is always the day after Christmas – it's actually always been the first weekday after Christmas, so that poor staff could enjoy time off. The enforced holiday perhaps replaced the need for the containers, Boxing Day replacing boxes. The fact that there was an increase in charitable donations anyway is partly thanks to the rise of philanthropic religious organizations, like the Salvation Army, who were also a key part in the redesign of Christmas as it became a festival focused on children.

If Dickens did reinvent Christmas, it was not focused on the Nativity at all. Dickens was a self-professed believer; Tolstoy called him "that great Christian writer", and the writer surely echoed Tiny Tim's observation: "God bless us, every one." Yet Christmas charity, as revived by Dickens, has maybe taken the place of Christianity at Christmas. Today those who say that we shouldn't forget "the true meaning of Christmas" often seem to mean either the importance of family or the joy of giving – both are at the heart of *A Christmas Carol.*

The Dickensian Christmas transcended class: aspirational for the poor and relatable for the rich. Whether in castle or workhouse, all enjoyed their Christmas rituals from dinner to gifts. The festival painted by Dickens was a great unifier.

Three kings of the nineteenth-century Christmas, and their gifts...

❖ *WASHINGTON IRVING...* The American brings the modern Christmas in from the cold. Reviving the cosiness of the classic country Christmas, his tales of roaring log fires spark Christmas nostalgia. Spreading Santa and snugness, Irving's gift is that warm sweet reviving feeling, mmmmyrrh.

❖ *PRINCE ALBERT...* The German brings old-world charm and nobility, to be emulated by all royal-watchers. So beloved is the Prince Consort that the customs he enacts, from Christmas trees to gingerbread and fruit and candle decorations, are copied throughout the land. Christmas cards with the royal couple's image are the height of fashion. When Albert skates at Christmas (rather well actually, certainly far better than Her Majesty), everyone skates. He even once rode a sleigh from London to Slough (of all the places – one hopes it was just so they could call it a Slough Ride...). Albert's gift is to host the sparkling royal Christmas that we all crave: pure festive gold.

✧ *CHARLES DICKENS…* The Englishman brings classic hot dishes to the Christmas table: not just mulled wine and Christmas pudding, but family cheer and a sense of community outreach. From his pages, you can almost inhale the scent of Cratchit cooking, the chill of crisp snow underfoot, and the homely aromas of Fred's Christmas party. Dickens' gift is a Christmas that tingles our senses – and if you don't agree, frankly I'm incensed.

MERRY CHRISTMAS!

Dickens gave the English language several familiar words and phrases in *A Christmas Carol*. Now we have a "Scrooge", as well as the anti-Christmas exclamation "Bah! Humbug!", plus the reformed Scrooge wishing the world a "Merry Christmas". Earlier he had said that, "If I could work my will… every idiot who goes about with 'Merry Christmas' on his lips should be boiled with his own pudding." Later of course Scrooge eats those words – not with any kind of pudding but as a side-dish of humble pie.

Speaking of pud, one of the earliest "Merry Christmas" greetings is in the song "We Wish You a Merry Christmas", sung door-to-door in the mummers' tradition of performing for money (or figgy pudding). No one quite knows when that song came about, though it pre-dates Dickens.

Possibly the earliest recorded use of the greeting was in 1565 as "Mery Christmas", though the more satisfying fuller phrase, "Merry Christmas and a Happy New Year", first appears in a 1699 letter written by an English admiral. There's then a gap, then Dickens brings the greeting back in his 1843 book. By chance that very same week, the greeting was also revived for the first commercial Christmas card.

THE CHRISTMAS CARD

Sir Henry Cole was a classic Victorian innovator and a very busy businessman. He wrote books on art, edited and published children's books, as well as having jurisdiction over the Great Exhibition, the London Museum, and various public properties that would become the Royal Albert Hall, the Victoria and Albert Museum, and the Royal College of Music. Oh, and public toilets.

So frantic was he, that Prince Albert once punned, "When you want steam, you must get Cole!" Sir Henry was instrumental in introducing the Penny Post, possibly even designing the world's first stamp, the Penny Black. The postal service didn't revolutionize life overnight, and it was only when the cost of posting a letter was slashed in 1840 that change was suddenly afoot. For the first time there was a new possibility for communication: the affordable mass mail-out.

Traditional Christmas missives had been popular for centuries – even the Romans were known to write seasonal greetings to each other. And here in the mid-nineteenth century, Christmas letters to loved ones were becoming more important, since industrialization had encouraged families to live further apart. Trains had made it possible to deliver such letters all the speedier. Yet in a fast-moving world, one of those fast-movers found no time to write these greetings. Sir Henry's overflowing postbox was a daily reminder of how bad he was at replying to his many friends and colleagues, who had used the postal service that he'd co-invented to wish him well at Christmas.

Greetings cards were already in use, with Valentine's and New Year's cards being quite popular. At this time of the year, schoolchildren would design Christmas "pieces" for their families, with a festive greeting on decorated notepaper. Sir Henry Cole was perfectly placed to try and combine these elements.

As a patron of the arts, Sir Henry asked a favourite member of the Royal Academy, John Calcott Horsley, to design a Christmas card for him, just for personal use. It would bear the greeting "A Merry Christmas and a Happy New Year to You", with a main picture of a family getting very merry on red wine. They raise a toast to the person viewing the card, and even the young children are having a good swig of the wine. That's right – the world's first Christmas card promoted underage drinking.

Horsley cleverly drew the main character in the picture a little like Sir Henry, which probably explains why his patron liked it so much. Unfortunately few others agreed. The portrait of the portly gent's family dinner was flanked by two side-panels showing the poor at Christmas. While the thought is there, the overflowing table in the centre is at odds with the poor figures pushed to either side. Meanwhile Dickens' contribution to the culture of charity was being finished exactly a mile to the north-east of Cole's print run at 12 Old Bond Street. The book was arguably the more inclusive of the two depictions, but both played their part in one of the most Christmas-changing Christmases we've known.

Sir Henry was so impressed by the product that he had 1,000 printed – and he didn't have 1,000 friends. So he took his share then sold the rest alongside illustrated children's books in the Old Bond Street shop. They were printed on stiff card, coloured by hand, and sold for a shilling. No jokes inside just yet – and none beeped "Jingle Bells" when you opened the card.

Six Christmas cards on history's mantelpiece...

✧ *HORSLEY & COLE'S* first picture… again. And again. Henry Cole persisted, publishing the same image each year till customers were won over. Within a few years the government had to hire in extra holiday staff for the

Christmas post. In the 1860s, colour printing became significantly cheaper, and Europe started sending too.

✧ *A BIT CHEAP...* In 1870 the half-penny stamp attracted those who couldn't afford cards before – though many still thought them tacky, with an 1877 letter to *The Times* newspaper calling the cards "a social evil".

✧ *THE CARD GAME...* In the early 1870s, printing firm Prang and Meyer mass-produced cards across England, and a year later spread to America. Within a decade their sales topped 5 million a year.

✧ *ANNIE GET YOUR CARD...* The world's first personalized Christmas card was sent from Scotland in 1891, featuring a cover pic of its sender: the world's most famous female sharpshooter. Annie Oakley was at the height of her fame, touring Scotland with Buffalo Bill's Wild West show. For the gunsmith later immortalized in the musical *Annie Get Your Gun*, there was indeed no business quite like showbusiness – and that meant spending Christmas in Glasgow, sending selfies back home. After all, anything Christmas cards could do, she could do better.

✧ *ROBINS BEST...* The red-breasted bird featured on many cards, possibly to warm to those delivering them: Victorian postmen were nicknamed "Robins" due to their red-trimmed uniform. (Or because thanks to the robbin' postman, my cards no longer have fivers in.)

✧ *CRIB SHEET...* Religious cards only hit doormats from the early twentieth century, and even then never outsold their secular shelf-mates. A 2010 survey of British supermarkets found just 0.8 per cent of Christmas cards looked cribwards.

PULL!

December 1843, with *A Christmas Carol* and the Christmas card, put London centre-stage as host of the modern Christmas. On 23 December that year, the *Illustrated London News* called Christmas "our old English anniversary of festivity and smiles". In Scotland it was barely celebrated, and throughout England and Wales, customs slowly spread, though London seemed to light each fuse… while everyone else waited to see if it went bang.

One such product was invented by London confectioner and wedding cake specialist Tom Smith. On holiday in Paris in the early 1840s, Smith was smitten by the packaging of some delightful sugared almond bonbons, delicately wrapped in wax paper with a twist at each end. Wrapping food – how very French. Smith's English upper-class clientele were always on the lookout for culinary fashion, so he combined these French fancies with the mottos from Chinese fortune cookies, and sold them at his shop on Clerkenwell's Goswell Road.

Ladies about town adored his exquisite bonbons, especially when hosting at Christmas. They were so popular in December that Smith spent the other eleven months thinking of new twists on the old formula. His customers couldn't wait to see what this year's innovation would be, from trinkets to firecrackers to party hats, later added by his son Walter. By rebranding them as party essentials, Smith made multiple sales per customer.

By the 1870s they were called "cosaques", named for the cracking sound like Cossack horsemen cracking their whips. A decade later, they became "crackers". Smith realized that the sweets were actually the least favourite part of the item, so the confectioner removed the confectionery. By the turn of the century, his factory sold 13 million crackers each Christmas – a genuine success story of Victorian entrepreneurship.

Eight things in your cracker and how far they've come...

- ✧ *THE TRINKETS*... Miniature presents from the early days of Tom Smith's new crackers, to impress his female clientele.

- ✧ *THE SWEET*... Less common today but if you do find one, merci to the French, who originally inspired the bonbon. Good, good. Bon bon.

- ✧ *THE BANG*... Sitting by the fire for inspiration, Smith heard the wood crackle as it burned. Eureka! He added what he called "bangs of expectation".

- ✧ *THE MOTTO*... Straight from the Chinese fortune cookie, they predicted the cracker-puller's New Year.

- ✧ *THE SEASONAL GREETINGS*... Got a little verse in your cracker? This dates back to Roman days.

- ✧ *THE JOKE*... Who knows where they get some of those jokes from. Then again, I'm one to talk.

- ✧ *THE PAPER CROWN*... The most recent arrival. When Twelfth Night parties went out of fashion, including the Lord of Misrule still directing the entertainment while wearing a mock crown, the popular crowns found a home in the cracker.

- ✧ *THE CARDBOARD BIT FROM A TOILET ROLL*... No idea.

THE HOLLY CART

Evergreens were easily accessible for country folk, but for the millions flocking to the cities, holly, ivy, and mistletoe were trickier to come by. For a while the "holly cart" provided the answer, with poorer folk trekking out of the cities to collect the plants for free, then trudging back through urban areas to sell for profit.

Ever the entrepreneur, cracker king Tom Smith spied a gap in the market. He instructed his already successful factory to produce paper decorations and tinsel, to replace the evergreens that had lasted for millennia. Still to this day our decorations are a tension between the two, with paper chains jostling with the evergreens for a place in our homes.

Not all evergreens were being pushed out though. In many ways they were just coming in – especially the biggest Christmas evergreen of all: the Christmas tree.

THE CHRISTMAS TREE TAKES ROOT

In amongst the astonishing levels of poverty, there was a burgeoning Victorian middle class, bringing the distant promise of social mobility. In the old days, society divided up into simply nobility and the rest. But now the English had a real sense of moving up – or down – in the world. There was an attitude of self-improvement, an enthusiasm for technology, and a love of fashion – and those who aimed high looked to the royals.

Thanks to kings from Hanover, the English knew of Christmas trees, popular in Germany since Martin Luther apparently deposited one in his lounge. British appearances were rarities; in 1789 a Mrs Papendiek wrote about having "an illuminated tree according to the German tradition" – but these were isolated occurrences, and Mrs Papendiek must have received odd looks.

In America too, locals were confused by German tendencies to become seasonal lumberjacks. American Revolutionary troops at Fort Dearborn in 1804 were baffled to see their German soldier-for-hire colleagues dragging firs from the forest. Pennsylvanian Germans continued the custom over the next few decades, but it remained a Germanic habit, until reports of the fashionable royal Christmases in England.

The first royal trees at Windsor Castle were not popular though, because the royals weren't popular. Christmas 1800 featured Queen Charlotte's enormous yew tree, recreating her German childhood custom. It was "about as high as any of us, lighted all over with small tapers, several little wax dolls among the branches in different places, and strings of almonds and raisins alternately tied from one to the other". Around the same time comes our first picture of a candlelit Christmas tree, at Wandsbek Castle in Hamburg.

Unfortunately, Queen Charlotte's husband George III was not well-liked, so their Christmas didn't catch on. Luckily for the tree, a royal heartthrob from Saxe-Coburg was just waiting in the wings.

VICTORIA AND ALBERT'S CHRISTMAS

In the early 1840s, Prince Albert made a concerted effort to share the traditional German Christmas with the public, and royal-watchers were quick to admire. As well as the giant tree at Windsor Castle, Albert also donated smaller trees to schools and army barracks.

Sometimes those royal German trees would look a tad, well, Australian – hung upside-down like a chandelier. They were still decorated with ribbons and pine cones, just rather scarily above the heads of Christmas revellers below. Another German custom had trees represented by wooden pyramids, but this was for poorer Germans.

The trees that Albert impressed on England were the full fir – and not one tree but hundreds. They might be mid-sized and hanging from the ceiling, or small and in the centre of tables of presents, laid out for the children on Christmas Eve rather than Christmas Day in the German custom. Presents would typically be doll figurines for the girls and swords and armour for the boys, and these became popular nationwide as the young royal family continued to advertise the perfect English Christmas.

Albert's "treenaissance" received a massive boost in 1848, when the *Illustrated London News* did what it did best: illustrate news, in London. A drawing of "The Queen's Christmas tree at Windsor Castle" showed the royal couple and their delighted children gawping at a tree fifteen feet tall. The picture was met with far greater acclaim than that image on the first Christmas card five years earlier: there was not a glass of wine or a drunk child in sight.

The picture of the young royals at play was republished in the United States two years later, although they removed the Queen's crown and Prince Albert's moustache in the hope of appealing to more Americans. De-royaled and de-Germanified, this may be one of the earliest examples of journalistic airbrushing. Photoshop, here we come. For the American reprint, let's give thanks to magazine editor Sarah Hale, who also first published "Mary Had a Little Lamb" and stories by Washington Irving and Edgar Allan Poe. She also had the idea for a national Thanksgiving Day, and campaigned in writing to each US president over 26 years, until Lincoln finally agreed. Thanks, Sarah.

In the same year as Hale's "tree-print", Dickens referred to the tree as "that pretty German toy". Its Germanic origins now lent it some exoticism, while in the past foreign customs hadn't spread so easily. It was the perfect time for the tree's breakthrough. America was softening its previously Puritan (or at least uncertain) stance on Christmas, and we've seen England lapping up new Christmas customs faster than you could say "humbug".

Three times our three kings of Christmas met...

✧ *WHEN ALBERT MET DICKENS...* The Prince Consort was a fan of Dickens, but the feeling was not mutual – simply because Dickens was in love with the Queen. On the royal wedding night at Windsor Castle in 1840, the already-married Dickens protested beneath the newlyweds' bedroom window by rolling around in the mud. Not surprisingly it was ineffective. In further protest, Dickens rudely refused all royal requests for an audience for the next three decades. The royal couple attended some of his performed readings, but Charles continued to turn down offers of honours, or a request to contribute to Albert's memorial fund after his demise. The Queen and the writer finally met, holding a cordial conversation, just weeks before Charles' death.

✧ *WHEN DICKENS MET IRVING...* The two writers admired each other greatly, and Dickens stayed at Irving's house in New York on 1 February 1842, during his American speaking tour. Irving's nostalgia for the classic Christmas inspired Dickens' writing, though the Englishman stopped short of the American's obsession with the Santa myth. Dickens was in no way interested in retelling or helping to spread Dutch legends. A Dickensian Christmas has the parents give the presents, while Irving's Christmas gives St Nick the credit.

✧ *WHEN IRVING MET ALBERT…* The consummate traveller had grown a little world-weary by the time he attended a royal ball in London in May 1842, but his overwhelm at the sight of the regalia was classically American. Adoring the pomp and ceremony, he was impressed by Prince Albert, whom he noted "speaks English very well". Ever the observer, Irving perceived that the Queen looked flushed and bothered by the entire event, continually adjusting her crown.

ARTIFICIAL TREES GROW

1851 saw the first Christmas tree ads in the *Illustrated London News*, and around the same time in New York, entrepreneur Mark Carr gave his fellow city-dwellers greater access to Christmas trees. Having taken two ox sleds to the Catskills and felled a few trees, he returned to the city to sell them – like the London holly cart except, being American, it was bigger. Carr started a whole industry: the Christmas tree lot. The Germans had started it, the English had popularized it – now the Americans were mass-marketing it.

Five years later, President Franklin Pierce installed the first White House Christmas tree; in 1923 Calvin Coolidge built on this tradition by making a ceremony out of lighting the tree.

Latin regions held out, especially Catholic countries suspicious of the tree's pagan origins. Northern Europe and North America were more Protestant, so the culture-swapping roots of their beloved tree were overlooked. Instead capitalist nations looked forward, which meant planning for the growing demand. Germany had deforestation concerns, so gradually a trend grew for mock trees made from goose feathers dyed green then attached to wire branches: the first artificial trees.

Worldwide tree demand was now in the millions, so if there were concerns for the forests, there should also have been concerns for the geese. So in the 1930s, the Addis Brush Company had a brainwave. That is, another brainwave – William Addis had already invented the toothbrush. Addis had surplus stocks of toilet brushes, which after careful remodelling could be sold as new artificial trees. Helpfully they were less flammable, at a time when candles were still being placed on many trees.

Aluminium trees arrived in the late 1950s, but left soon afterwards as they looked too fake. 1965's *A Charlie Brown Christmas* killed off the aluminium tree for good, with Charlie's love for the real tree – even just a poor-looking sapling – winning hearts across America. Since then, the artificial tree has tried to look real, though those toilet brush branches are a lot sturdier – very handy when supporting the ornaments that were becoming quite the fashion.

FOUR CANDLES

The doors were now open to German Christmas craft. The evergreens of old were now intermingled with coloured paper, oranges, nuts, biscuits, and handcrafted festive greetings, spelled out in flower petals or leaves. This latter custom was popular in church as well as at home. Many of the items had been used in decoration before, but the German touch was to craft their use very deliberately. The greenery was more carefully trimmed, the colours were more uniform, and the décor was more edible.

The Advent wreath was one example. Popular already in Germany and based on ancient Roman decoration, it became popular throughout Europe. This evergreen circle of life had four candles (no, not handles for forks) to be lit each Sunday in Advent, then possibly a fifth on Christmas Day. The wreath we keep on our doors each year has lost the candles – the flames never lasted long in December weather anyway.

I'M FOREVER BLOWING BAUBLES

Christmas markets blossomed throughout Europe in the 1870s, including a new guest stall that cropped up entirely by accident. Some Bohemian glass-blowers were cooling down with a beverage or two after a hot day at the furnace, and challenged each other to a bubble-blowing contest – biggest bubble wins. Fun and games over, they returned to work – but amid the empty tankards were the leftover glass bubbles. The blowers' wives spotted them and sold them in markets as "spirit balls". They were hung in doorways to ward off the "evil eye" – the perfectly rounded reflection meant that you could see evil coming in all directions.

They were too heavy for real tree branches, and stronger artificial trees were still a way off yet. Once new gas technology meant that smaller baubles could be blown with greater accuracy, they found a home with the paper chains and tinsel on the branches of the tree.

With European craft markets devouring these new decorations, innovation looked back to move forward. Anything too outrageous wouldn't catch on, so they looked to the Christmas crib for inspiration. It had vanished amid Puritan accusations of idolatry, but Christmas was now such big business that public demand trumped those claims. Finely sculpted crib scenes were made in Europe once again then shipped to Britain and America. Harking back to an alleged heyday of their production, these new ones were far more popular than they had ever been claimed to be.

ANGEL VS FAIRY

Till now the tin-gold angel still sat at the top of the tree, a disguised infant Christ to get past the pious arbitrators. But that too was now updated by the unstoppable Christmas craft industry. Rather than the old-fashioned tin, it was now a wax doll, or made of porcelain, a favourite of the young Victoria. By adding delicate clothing, there was extra scope for the doll to be played with after Christmas – after all, craft-makers were now embracing a Christmas of children and toys. The tin-gold angel was male, but the new dolls were targeted at girls, so the gender changed. So the Nativity role had to change too – no longer would it be the infant Jesus, but an angel, possibly Gabriel (who was male… but then do angels have a gender? That's for another time).

The shift coincided with the rise of the popular family Christmas pantomime, where the protective Good Fairy was becoming a much-loved figure. She was a theatrical bridge between other characters and the audience, assuring that all would work out alright in the end (and if it didn't, it wasn't the end). If you can have a protective Good Fairy on the Christmas stage, you can have one on the Christmas tree. So as the new doll topped the tree, some chose to call her an angel, and some a fairy. Which is it for you? If you still call yours "the tin-gold angel representing the infant Jesus", then well done, award yourself ten Christmas nostalgia points. Actually, make it twelve.

THE YULE LOG BURNS OUT

As anyone who's ever put up a tree knows, they take up more room than you think. So with world domination achieved by the Christmas tree (I think there was a *Doctor Who* episode about that once), something else would be edged out.

For centuries, the Yule log had adapted and thrived – the only way to survive as a Christmas custom. When it wanted to be Scandinavian, it was more Scandinavian than Nordic jumpers. When it wanted to be accepted by the church, it claimed to represent keeping the stable warm for the baby Jesus. When the church frowned upon Christmas heresy, the log quietly returned to being secular again. But the tree naturally replaces the log, so the log that had started burning long before Christ's birth finally began to flicker out.

Hang on a second, I hear you wassail – there's plenty of room in this inn! If our Christmas can house Santa, Scrooge, *and* Jesus, if we can accommodate holly, ivy, mistletoe, *and* tinsel, if the tree can support an angel *and* a fairy without toppling (oh, and a star, and a bow in some places – and I've even heard of someone who religiously puts up a doughnut), then surely we can fit a little Yule log next to the tree?

Ah, well there we have our answer – it wasn't little, and fireplaces were shrinking. Smaller city housing had fireplaces at least half the size of centuries before – and those popular Yule logs were big enough to burn for the full twelve days. Once in the home, the simple tree was far lower maintenance too. Though admit it – we miss our log fires.

Across Europe, some were less inclined to drop their logs so quickly. The French took a few extra decades before they warmed to the tree, so they clung to the dear old Yule log. But here too, city culture was the future. Small fireplaces, inaccessible woodland, and the increased fire risk all led to urbanites needing a new way to represent their beloved logs.

If there isn't a French saying, "When in trouble, make confectionery", then there should be. Enterprising bakers reminded Parisians of their Christmas logs by immortalizing them in chocolate form, as the *Bûche de Noël*: the chocolate log.

THE TWELVE FORTY SOME DAYS OF CHRISTMAS

With the Yule log fizzling out, other old customs had to prove their worth. Twelfth Night was still a popular celebration, but it was rather adult and boisterous. Did it fit with Christmas' new child-centric nature? The Lord of Misrule from medieval days now reigned on Twelfth Night, with a mock king and queen chosen by a pea or bean in the Twelfth Cake (it was largely fixed – nothing kills a party like Tiny Tom or Great Aunt Doris becoming party host). The Lord for the night would be dusted with soot and given a paper party crown, yet to find its way into Tom Smith's crackers. There might even be a cobbled-together sceptre and full fake regalia for their temporary role.

By the 1870s, Queen Victoria reined in such celebrations. It coincided with a few other seasonal shifts: as we've seen, Boxing Day became a bank holiday in 1871. If you wanted a raucous Christmas celebration, Christmas Eve was proving a busy night in the pubs, and to sober up, Hyde Park's Serpentine Lake hosted its annual Christmas morning swim from 1864. Brrr…

With no Twelfth Night party, the popular Twelfth Cake became Christmas cake, or was replaced by Christmas pudding. The bean in the cake was no longer needed, with no Lord of Misrule to elect – so the coin in the Christmas pudding was all that remained. All sorts had been stirred into Christmas puddings by this point: a ring to predict wedding bells, a thimble for a blessed life, even a good-luck horseshoe (not so lucky if the horse was still attached). Today, whoever is served that coin is no longer the Lord of Misrule, just lucky enough to get the coin.

EPIPHANY AND CANDLEMAS

The English may have lost their Twelfth Night, but north of the border, the Scots were enjoying their Hogmanay. Particular

New Year customs developed, including "first-footing": the superstition that the first person over the threshold each year brings great luck... if they fit the right description. It's bad luck for it to be a woman, and I know how horribly unfair that sounds, because it's also bad luck for the first-footer to have red hair, a squint, or flat feet – and unfortunately I think I've got all three.

By largely ignoring Christmas since the Reformation, the Scots' winter festival grew a flavour of its own, keeping the religious Christmas and the secular shenanigans well and truly separate. On this issue, the English had become wrapped up in knots like an "Auld Lang Syne" handshake: how to separate raucous Twelfth Night celebrations from the church's Epiphany, commemorating the wise men's holy visit? In the past, presents were given to emulate the Magi's gifts, but with England's royals and America's Santa Claus focusing their giving on Christmas Eve or Christmas Day (and money running out by January), Epiphany was no longer appropriate for gift exchanges, unless it was in a shop with a receipt.

Victorian decoration and commerce shifted the entire season earlier. The old days when Christmas was celebrated through Twelfth Night and on till Candlemas were long gone. Candlemas clings on in some churches, and still has a place as a secular festival in the United States, signifying the end of winter, potentially, if the groundhog doesn't see its shadow. The second of February is indeed Groundhog Day (and so's the next day, and the next day, and the day after that...).

By the end of the nineteenth century, 2 February seemed late to end Christmas. It may have worked when you only started celebrating on Christmas Eve, but the decorations and tree look tired by early January if they've been up since early December. Instead that month-and-a-week Christmas season shifted from being 24 December till 2 February, to approximately 1 December till 6 January. Advent and the Twelve Days would suffice for decorations, surely.

Even today, where shops play Christmas music from 1 November, we adhere domestically to these dates. By chance I write this chapter on 1 December. When I left my house this morning, the only decorations were in shops. Climbing the hill home at a dark five o'clock, a quarter of my street is now illuminated, as of today. I note that each of these homes is occupied by my retired neighbours; the families and commuters will take another few days to get around to it, I assume. Or is it that the older folks are more likely to uphold tradition?

TURKEY'S CROWN

By the end of Victoria's reign, roast turkey ruled the roost on the Christmas dinner table – though the queen herself was not the biggest fan. When she took the throne back in 1837, turkey was far too expensive, so beef was the traditional Christmas roast in the north and goose in the south, or rabbit for the poor. Victoria sided with the north on this one.

She did of course find a variety of meats placed in front of her each Christmas, including exotic birds like swan, snipe, or capercaillie. In 1851 the royal menu contained turkey for the first time, and once again that meant that the nation would copy. Thanks to Victorian methods of mass production, this was now possible at an affordable cost.

Over in Norfolk, these turkeys would be raised with the sole aim of the Christmas dinner plate. So how to get hundreds of turkeys from Norfolk to London in time? Simple. Starting in October each year, you make them walk to, yes, their own execution. This annual procession of the doomed birds was quite a sight, especially thanks to the shoes they wore. To protect their feet, each turkey had hard-wearing leather boots for the 100-mile one-way commute to market. At least they had a big meal waiting for them in London; the weary birds were fattened up in time for Christmas.

A Finger-lickin' Tradition

No Christmas custom is ever global. Present-day Japan for example doesn't have turkey or goose or even the lesser-spotted capercaillie… they have a KFC bucket. It's a very modern Christmas custom, but a custom nonetheless. In 1974 some American visitors struggled to find any turkey in Japan so they tried the newly opened Kentucky Fried Chicken. Spying a gap in the market (and a white beard that made Colonel Sanders look a bit Santa-like), the company started a "Kentucky For Christmas" campaign (still conveniently spelling KFC).

This Christmas, millions of Japanese diners will queue around the block to collect their specially ordered bucket of cake, wine, and of course southern-fried chicken. When you can't get turkey, you can always rely on the Colonel.

The Victorian era paved the way for the mass-market Christmas. Ever since, capitalism has been waiting in the wings for any hint of a gap in the market – and sometimes not waiting in the wings but barging out and interrupting the rather sweet solo that a chorister was singing.

As the nineteenth century drew to a close, Christmas found a new battle on its hands. It had struggled for survival after Puritanism, and won. Thanks to Santa and Scrooge, Christmas was here to stay – and we now can't conceive of a world without it. Now though it had to fight for its soul: was there a place for Christmas in church, or just in the stores? Plus, beyond its own battle, it had another role to play, in war.

Photograph of soldiers playing football in no man's land during the Christmas truce, December 1914

Chapter 10

A Lesson in War

(1862–1928)

With industrialization came the rise (and rise, and my word there are a lot of floors in this place) of department stores, heralding that frequent festive duel: immaterial spirituality versus material Buzz Lightyear toys. Capitalism has certainly helped Christmas – it's partly thanks to the big stores that Christmas was becoming so child-centric, and without this, I'd never have got that Scalextric set when I was eight. And hey, maybe in among the toys, kids are puzzling out whether Christmas is about infinity, or beyond.

In this chapter, we'll explore commercialism, the church finally claiming carolling for themselves, and how The Great War changed Christmas.

OPEN FOR BUSINESS

Macy's of New York was one of the first department stores, and indeed one of the first to seize on Christmas. In 1862 Rowland Hussey Macy himself decided that an in-store Santa Claus would be perfect for children to visit and thus create more footfall. His store was also one of the first to offer a money-back guarantee, and the first to have a Christmas window display: originally a collection of porcelain dolls and a recreation of scenes from *Uncle Tom's Cabin*.

Just decades before, such a thing would have been unthinkable – because we take it for granted that shops have windows at all. Only in the late nineteenth century was plate glass available for large shops to display their merchandise to the outside world. Until that point, you knew what the shop stocked, you went in, and you selected your wares. With windows, a new optimistic hobby was accidentally created: window-shopping.

These innovations drifted over the Atlantic; 1888 saw the first in-store Santa's grotto, in J. P. Robert's East London shop. A decade later and a few miles west, Selfridge's opened (not just selling fridges), with Gordon Selfridge importing the window displays he'd worked on in his Chicago apprenticeship. They were the talk of London, to the point that rival stores like Harrods tried to outdo them. Selfridge coined the expression "only X shopping days to Christmas", contributing to the rise of customer expectation each Christmas (though he would put the appropriate, ever-decreasing number there instead of the letter X).

America was experiencing competitive window décor too, with onlookers blocking the street to get a look. Window-shoppers travelled for hours just to see these free displays, without ever once entering the shop. The pastime grew more popular through the twentieth century, causing the new notion of "Christmas creep". The season started earlier and earlier in-store: displays up, lights on, offers on. London's famed Oxford Street lights were switched on a full three weeks earlier in the 1990s than in the 1950s.

Thanks to electricity, these visitors didn't even have to be there during the day – after all, most of them weren't buying anything. They could do a day's work then come into town with their families, tour around the exterior of several department stores before going home without spending anything. With electric light, these displays looked more impressive than ever, some having been worked on all year. In time, artists from Salvador Dali to Andy Warhol helped create window displays. Those stores not blessed by world-renowned artists benefitted from technological advancements: mechanical characters, rising platforms, and frosted snow scenes were mainstays of stores in London, New York, and Chicago. In the 1950s, Woodward & Lothrop's of Washington D.C. even featured live penguins in their window. Electricity also meant another commercial bonus: late-night shopping.

THE LIGHT OF THE WORLD?

At home too, electricity was a Christmas transformer. Thomas Edison marketed lightbulbs from 1879, and three years later his employee Edward Johnson used them in a string of lights to decorate the family Christmas tree – in good ol' American red, white, and blue. They were their own advertisement, illuminating his window for his neighbours to see. What will those crazy Edison employees think of next? Well, flashing lights. Johnson's neighbours were blown away. Not literally – in fact these lights slowly helped stop the all-too-frequent fires courtesy of the pretty yet unfortunate combination of flammable trees, candles, and ornate paper.

Elsewhere and apparently unknowing of this, telephonist Ralph Morris was inspired by the lights flickering on his switchboard as people dialled in. What a perfect addition to the Christmas decorations, he thought – and safer than candles. His son had recently suffered burns, and a decade earlier a Chicago hospital had burned to the ground due to decorative candles on a flammable tree. In 1908, insurance companies tried to ban Christmas candles for this very reason.

The new lights remained unaffordable for most people until after World War II, but over time the electric lights were steadily extinguishing candles all but for good. Could it be at this point that Christmas started to lose a bit of Christ? Candles had signified Jesus as the "light of the world", although the flame's mystic significance dated back to pagans rolling that fiery wheel into the sea. In the twentieth century, the candlelight finally flickered out. All that remain in the twenty-first are the Advent candles, those in Christingle oranges, or those aromatic ones passed around as gifts till the use-by date finally sees them off.

THE ADVENT OF ADVENT

The church was losing its grip on Christmas. It no longer held the starting-pistol for the season – for many it now began not with the start of Advent, but with the appearance of the festive window displays in the new churches of commercialism, the department stores.

For the church, the beginning of Advent has always been Advent Sunday, four Sundays before Christmas – meaning as early as 27 November or as late as 3 December. Each Sunday, one of four candles would be lit in the Advent wreath. Some churches devote each of the four Sundays to the patriarchs, the prophets, John the Baptist, and Mary – all related to the coming of Jesus. It's cheerier than the previous four themes: sermons on death, judgment, heaven, and hell that used to feature on the Sundays of Advent.

If you think Advent starts on 1 December, that's all down to commercialism, which couldn't let the church have Advent to itself. This standardization is all thanks to the Advent calendar, which like so many festive innovations, came from Germany.

Seven Advent calendars...

✧   *THE PRE-CALENDAR*... Advent was celebrated from at least the fifth century, and by the start of the twentieth century, candles and wreaths were popular. Protestant German families marked a chalk line each day till Christmas Eve – a bit like caricatures of prison life.

✧   *THE HOMEMADE CALENDAR*... began life in the 1850s, each one personalized. One Mrs Lang made calendars with sweets on string for her son Gerhard, who loved Advent, probably because he was allowed a sweet a day.

✦ *ANOTHER DOOR OPENS...* Gerhard grew up and mass-produced Advent calendars from 1908. Around the same time, newspapers offered them as free gifts – so Gerhard upped his game, or his calendars' days were numbered. Which was kind of the point. Gerhard was the first to add cardboard doors, with a picture or Bible verse behind each.

✦ *A NEW START...* for Advent in the 1920s, as Gerhard decided that a 1 December start day would save redesigning the calendars each year.

✦ *THE COUNTDOWN STOPS...* Rationing ceased production, but the calendars returned after World War II to great acclaim, Lang's calendars opening doors all over the world.

✦ *I LIKE IKE, IKE LIKES ADVENT CALENDARS...* Just as a pic of Victoria and Albert brought the Christmas tree to the United States, President Eisenhower helped spread the Advent calendar in a photo of him giving them to his grandchildren.

✦ *ALL I WANT FOR CHRISTMAS IS MY TWO FRONT TEETH...* Chocolate joined the calendars in the 1950s. Consumers had a choice between chocolate and Bible verses – guess which sold better? Once again, a burgeoning Christian custom was no match for festive gorging. And all because of those ridiculous commercial pictures in magazines and newspapers, can't stand 'em... Sorry, just an ad vent.

NOSTALGIA'S NOT WHAT IT USED TO BE

The church spent centuries trying to puzzle out if it should celebrate Christmas or not – but the commercial world of the early twentieth century didn't take so long to deliberate. As shoppers were shopping, they could see that Christmas had changed beyond recognition. Queen Victoria had died and Christmas had changed – cause and effect, so it seemed.

A wave of instant nostalgia crept in: the Victorian Christmas seemed like the classic Christmas, even if it had only just ended. Stores gladly stepped in with Victoriana to meet that demand. Once again Christmas trends were harking back to times that may never have been as rosy as they were being painted.

As ever in Christmas innovation, it was individuals with ideas who rang the changes. So in the late years of Victoria's reign, one clergyman concocted a new plan to reclaim a corner of Christmas for the church.

LESSONS AND GHOST STORIES

Edward Benson was a schoolmaster at Rugby school, arriving soon after it popularized the sport of rugby football. He was hand-selected by Prince Albert to be Head at the new Wellington College, before moving to a variety of church roles as an ordained deacon, becoming Bishop of Truro in Cornwall in 1877. He went on to become Archbishop of Canterbury, and to influence Christmas literature by telling his friend Henry James a simple ghost story, developed by the writer into festive favourite *The Turn of the Screw*. In that way that Victorian society people appeared to, Benson left creative successes all over the place: one of his sons went on to write the *Mapp and Lucia* novels, another wrote the lyrics to "Land of Hope and Glory". But in terms of Christmas, Bishop Benson had a major impact all on his own.

On our tenth date of Christmas…
(Truro, 24 December 1880)

Bishop Benson waits in the doorway of the shack, wondering if anyone even recognizes this as their temporary cathedral. Truro's sixteenth-century parish church was much-loved before its demolition, and getting locals on side with the new building project has proven tricky. Seven months on and they have a large wooden shed with benches: a humble way of celebrating that humble first Christmas. The fear is that the benches might remain empty.

In the pub over the road, Benson can hear a little too much Christmas carousing. They're celebrating time off work rather than the birth of Christ, but hopefully his new carol service might coax a few in, especially those who enjoy a good sing-song after a few drinks.

More than ever, the carol seems to be a uniquely English property, whether or not that's true. Especially here in Cornwall, many have been concerned that the old folk carols would be lost forever – but the local pubs have shaken with the sound of renewed carolling lately. Let us see if they can be lured from building to building.

Benson's father used a similar format to this service, assembling ancient sources into a complete service for Christmas Eve. Through a conversation with his friend Somerset Walpole (future Bishop of Edinburgh) Benson has reassembled this idea.

By half past nine, a few familiar churchgoers enter. Bishop Benson nods – but he's hoping for newcomers. He's modelled this service on the medieval feast days, when a church would present nine lessons. He's selected nine passages spanning Old and New Testaments, a bluffer's guide from original sin to Jesus' birth. He's chosen carols and other pieces of music, including popular anthems from Handel's Messiah. *This is squarely aimed at the regular Denzil, rather than trying to be high art or high church.*

Shortly before ten o'clock at night, that pub door opens: out tumble several men a little worse for wear. Some clergy would turn them away, but this is aimed at them. Benson hands them a service sheet, and in they go.

The service is a triumph. Readings are given by successive church staff from chorister upwards to Benson himself for the closing lesson. Songs include "The First Nowell", "Good Christian Men Rejoice", and "O Come, All Ye Faithful" – familiar even to those who've never stepped into a church in their life, or fallen into one.

CORNWALL TO CAMBRIDGE

The service ran from 10:05 to 11:15 p.m., and the benches were full. The church faithful enjoyed the theology, the newcomers enjoyed the format (and the singing). The men's choir gave their all, and friends and neighbours communed together as one. The wooden shack was eventually removed and the real cathedral now stands there, impressively topped with three spires and a green copper roof. That temporary shack became a shoe factory in Redruth in west Cornwall.

Other churches copied the service, and so it grew. Two years later, the *West Briton & Cornwall Advertiser* remarked that Christmas carols were a "department of folklore which has richly repaid the attention that has been given to it of late", and thanks to Benson's format, they had a new life.

From a shed to one of the most ornate buildings in the country – it would take a Cambridge college to fully hone the format into the one we're familiar with today. Benson's service began with

"The Lord at First Had Adam Made"; decades later it would begin with "Once in Royal David's City". When Cambridge took up the mantle, it was in tribute to those who had fallen in the Great War.

CHRISTMAS IN THE TRENCHES

Christmas Day wasn't just a theoretical day of peace. It had been in practice too. Up until the fifteenth century, the accepted rule was that there would be no fighting on Christmas Day. Even before Christ, ancient Rome's winter celebrations were held in the "home" season, when troops returned to their families for the cold months. No act of war could be declared, though existent wars would still be fought.

War in the twentieth century was on such a vast scale, fought on so many fronts, that no such civility was officially extended. The Great War began in August 1914 and many spread that optimistic soundbite that it would be "over by Christmas". By November it was clear that this was far from likely; the war was far bloodier than predicted.

In the run-up to Christmas, Pope Benedict XV suggested a one-day truce: "the guns may fall silent at least upon the night the angels sang." High Command disagreed. Orders came down to the trenches of northern France that troops should treat Christmas as any other day. No major offensives were planned, so that day could proceed hopefully easier than most, and on the German side too, the order was to fight on. Echoing the decree from Cromwell's Puritan government three centuries earlier, Christmas would be cancelled – and similar unrest, then defiance, ensued.

Some acknowledgment of Christmas was not only permitted but encouraged. All sides were ordered to decorate their trenches – a little visual reminder of what they were fighting for, and to encourage them to keep fighting harder. There were parcels and letters, including Christmas cards from the king to every soldier, as well as handmade paper decorations and simple Christmas presents. German troops near Ypres went further: small Christmas trees and hampers of favourite treats made their way to the trenches. Many trenches became more decorated than had been sanctioned.

It was meant to hark back to home, but instead it reminded many of Christmas peace. This miniature Christmas cut through the barbarism and caused soldiers to question the pointlessness of killing strangers just a few feet away, celebrating exactly the same thing. There was an unseen mutual respect. Even before Christmas, there were informal agreements of quiet time where no shots would be fired, if only to recover bodies from the battlefield. There were brief conversations, sometimes including cigarette bartering.

ONE SILENT NIGHT

Christmas Eve saw the first aerial bomb drop on Britain, at Dover Castle. In the trenches though, the glow of candlelight could be seen across no man's land. Some of the German Christmas trees made their way from the tabletops below to ground level. Perhaps inevitably, the Germans starting singing carols at midnight, and the British joined in. Evening singing was not uncommon in the trenches and the proximity meant that soldiers would frequently hear each other's songs. Only now of course, it was a carol.

The tune was familiar to the British, even if the words were German. As "Stille Nacht" drifted over the trenches, the English joined in with "Silent Night", exactly ninety-six years to the day after its composition in a church 400 miles to the southeast. Further carols were sung in English and German, until heads on both sides poked above the parapet, then trusting individuals stepped into no man's land. Hands were shaken, and Christmas dinner rations were salvaged to make gifts: German sausages were swapped for British plum puddings, and cigars and cigarettes were exchanged. Other nationalities joined in with their songs; Captain Sir Edward Hulse noted that the songs "ended up with 'Auld Lang Syne' which we all, English, Scots, Irish, Prussians, Wurttenbergers, etc, joined in. It was absolutely astounding, and if I had seen it on a cinematograph film I should have sworn that it was faked!"

FESTIVE FOOTBALL

The next morning, encouraged by the carolling of the night before, shouts of "Merry Christmas, Tommy!" emanated from the German trenches. Now in daylight they ventured to greet their neighbours again, taking photos with each other and showing pictures of loved ones back home. Some parts saw informal kickabouts, if not a full-fledged football match (though the image appeals, thanks to the grumblings of Corporal Edmund Blackadder that he was never offside. When writer Robert Graves fictionalized the match, he gave the final score as 3–2 to the Germans).

Though Christmas Eve had opened the lines of communication, the Christmas Day meeting was the more rebellious, at least in the eyes of their superiors. A rousing song was one thing, but seeing the faces of those left back home was not going to help triggers be pulled. Previous fraternization had been isolated; now it was scores of men. And there was no end in sight – no agreement that these friendly encounters were just for one day. For weeks now, some sections of the front line had seen British–German relations being a little too cordial. On 1 December, a German sergeant had swung by a British trench "to see how we were getting on".

Private Henry Williamson of the London Rifle Brigade wrote a Boxing Day letter home:

> *Dear Mother, I am writing from the trenches. It is 11 o'clock in the morning… In my mouth is a pipe presented by the Princess Mary. In the pipe is tobacco. Of course, you say. But wait. In the pipe is German tobacco. Haha, you say, from a prisoner or found in a captured trench. Oh dear, no! From a German soldier. Yes a live German soldier from his own trench. Yesterday the British & Germans met & shook hands in the Ground between the trenches, & exchanged souvenirs, & shook hands. Yes, all day Xmas day, & as I write. Marvellous, isn't it?*

Williamson went on to write over sixty books, including the nature novel *Tarka the Otter*.

RETURNING TO WAR

It was far from marvellous for High Command, who were beginning to become concerned that this truce was growing. It took days to fully realize the gravity and scale of the problem: up to 100,000 troops involved in the unofficial ceasefire. For war, it was vital that one's enemy should be kept as "the other". In a week when one German soldier accidentally fired a gun and then wrote to the British to apologize, this ceasefire had clearly gone too far.

The truce was certainly not all-encompassing; the front line was long. Some areas saw bloody combat on Christmas Day. Some had heard of the Christmas truce, put their head above the parapet in greeting, and been shot and killed. Belgian, French, and Indian troops were generally baffled by the behaviour of the British and German encounters, though they too were becoming drawn into the conviviality. Even in the thick of the friendliness, there were those who daren't leave the trenches for fear of being shot at, or who opposed the idea of a truce. The latter opinion was held by at least one corporal: the young Adolf Hitler. But the isolated incidents were beginning to spread.

For most, it was a one-day truce, the agreement being no shots fired till Christmas Day midnight. In some areas though, the artillery fire fell silent all through Christmas week and into New Year. There were reports of brief joint religious services. One English machine gunner, a hairdresser back home, gave haircuts to German soldiers. They kneeled on the ground as their barber dutifully took clippers to his sworn enemies' necks.

The authorities stepped up the consequences to prevent future outbreaks of peace, and sent the soldiers back to work. Court martials were threatened for any future fraternization. Easter 1915 saw a further attempt at a truce, and again each December through the war. Each request seems to have come from the German side, with the British rebuffing each time for fear of High Command's response. The "live and let live" attitude occasionally raised its head above the parapet, but never in the same way as on Christmas Eve and Christmas Day 1914.

The moving events of the Great War's truce could so easily have been one of this book's twelve key dates across the history of Christmas. Sadly though, it didn't change very much – war is with us more than ever today; there has been war somewhere in the world each Christmas since that truce. World peace is something we put on our Christmas list, but seems to be temporarily unavailable. Now without trench warfare and without a front line, it is all too easy to think of the enemy not as neighbours, but as strangers a world away. When a soldier can fire a weapon from the Pentagon and it can fire in Syria, there is no day off for Christmas.

Six Christmas military manoeuvres...

✧ 1553: The Battle of Tucapel: Rebels defeat Spanish conquistadors and execute the Chilean governor.

✧ 1776: George Washington leads his Continental Army across the Delaware river on Christmas Day night, to ambush Britain's Hessian troops at Trenton, New Jersey. Washington's men include future US president James Monroe and future Founding Father, ten-dollar-bill centrefold, and star of Broadway, Alexander Hamilton.

✧ 1837: The Battle of Lake Okeechobee: US General Zachary Taylor leads 1,000 troops against the Seminoles.

✧ 1941: Japanese occupation begins after the Battle of Hong Kong ends. Meanwhile the Free French Forces liberate the first piece of French land: the archipelago of Saint Pierre and Miquelon.

✧ 1968: Kilvenmani massacre: 44 "untouchable" women and children die when Kizhavenmani village is burned down, after their request for higher wages.

✧ 1989: Former Romanian President Nicolae Ceauescu and his wife Elena are tried for genocide and summarily executed, two weeks before Romania abolishes capital punishment.

GOING UP TO CAMBRIDGE

Eric Milner-White was senior chaplain to the 7th Infantry Division, and received the Distinguished Service Order in the 1918 New Year Honours' List. On his return, he resumed his former place of work, as chaplain and now Dean and Fellow of King's College, Cambridge.

His return to Civvy Street brought a fresh approach to his role. He knew that after the war there needed to be healing and reconciliation, with a focus on pre-war days. His experiences also gave him a new zest for imaginative worship, to engage the returning troops. With Christmas approaching, Bishop Benson's Lessons and Carols service was the perfect format for a festive service. He sought to retain this but add new elements. Working with college organist Arthur Henry Mann as music director, they decided that choral scholars and older Lay Clerks from the college would make up the choir, as instructed by its founder Henry VI over 400 years earlier. He'd long since passed on, but when a king orders, you obey.

The revised service took place on Christmas Eve 1918 and was an instant success. Originally it featured a carol from each century from the fourteenth onwards, though over time it became clear that many popular carols came from the eighteenth and nineteenth centuries.

The repeat event in 1919 saw some changes, including popular carol "Once in Royal David's City" starting the service. It would take some years before it was sung by a solo boy's voice. To avoid undue panic, the chosen chorister is still only told just before the service begins. The song list has changed over the years, no two years being the same. The skeleton structure of carols interspersed with lessons and prayers, read by ascending ranks, remains unchanged.

NINE LESSONS AND CAROLS, FOUR CORNERS OF THE WORLD

For many, the Nine Lessons and Carols service is the full English, even though some of its compositions come from across Europe and even America and Australia. The post-Great War origins of the Cambridge version gave it an air of patriotism. Indeed it was just after the next war, in 1946, that composer Ralph Vaughan Williams suggested that the Nine Lessons and Carols service should be even more English, starting with home-born classic "God Rest Ye Merry, Gentlemen" and concluding with "The First Nowell".

There was an attempt at English ownership of carols throughout the century, especially with *The Oxford Book of Carols* in 1928, edited by Vaughan Williams, who also co-founded the English Folk Dance and Song Society. Like Davies Gilbert MP and William Sandys a century earlier, it was down to folk connoisseurs and historians to preserve and promote carols. Vaughan Williams especially preferred to publish Victorian carols with less sentimental, less Germanic folk tunes than they would have been sung with. His claim was clear: the carols belonged to Blighty.

The same year as that book's publication, there was another giant leap for Britain's carol heritage, as BBC radio broadcast "A Festival of Nine Lessons and Carols", a.k.a. *Carols from King's*, for the first time. Even in wartime, when the chapel's glass was removed for the war effort, a very chilly service still continued. As well as the glass, the name "King's" was removed for security reasons.

The broadcast went international in the 1930s and the world has heard *Carols from King's* each Christmas Eve since. For many it heralds not the start of the commercial Christmas, but of the domestic or spiritual Christmas. Especially for Britons far from home, the international broadcast has brought them back home, whether at Everest base camp or in the Gobi desert. In millions of British homes, it's the soundtrack to last-minute vegetable-chopping or present-wrapping.

The television and radio broadcast differ; the televised version is pre-recorded earlier in December (and contains two fewer lessons), while the radio version is live – and therefore extra magical. Across the world, churches and other buildings have emulated the event; the US equivalent has been held at Groton School, Massachusetts since 1928.

The invention of broadcasting sent Christmas traditions across the world faster than Annie Oakley's Christmas card, and nearly as fast as one of her bullets. Dickens wrote of the extremities of a lighthouse keeper and a ship at sea: far and lonely Christmases shown to Scrooge by the Ghost of Christmas Present. Even they could now be reached at Christmas – all they needed was a wireless radio.

Cover of the second Christmas edition of the
Radio Times, 19 December 1924

Chapter 11

Through the Marvels of
Modern Science

(1906–2012)

The British empire spread its exports wherever it reached: milky tea, railways, buttoned-up repression, zero attempt to learn the *lingua franca*, and Christianity. It promoted an English Christmas that was actually a mixed stocking of carols, trees, and decorations – customs baked elsewhere, but sprinkled with English seasoning. German, Roman, and Scandinavian oddments cropped up in India, Africa, and far-flung islands. The sun never set on the British empire, just as the Yule log never stopped burning, until it did.

To remind folks of home, the celebrations were often themed on royal Christmases of the past: Tudor, Stuart, or Victorian. *A Christmas Play before Queen Elizabeth* was one of the festive talking-points of 1858. *The Sydney Daily Telegraph* reported in 1879: "Once more the Christmas season, with all its pleasing memories, is upon us – welcome, as it always is wherever an English-speaking community is gathered together."

Radio broadcasting helped sell the unquestionably English brand of Christmas even further. In this chapter, the chimes of Big Ben will echo around the world, tolling and telling of royally London-centric festivities.

ONE LESSON AND CAROL – ON AIR

Broadcasting was developed by pioneers with now familiar surnames: Morse, Hertz, Ohm, Ampère, Volta, and Marconi. The first transmission of any radio entertainment programme was on Christmas Eve 1906: a one-man impromptu carol service courtesy of Reginald Fessenden, Canadian inventor and amateur violinist.

He transmitted a demonstration to ships' radio operators (known as "sparks") from Brank Rock, Massachusetts. Instead of the usual Morse code weather updates and time signals, receivers heard a brief burst of Fessenden reading Luke's Nativity account, performing "O Holy Night" on violin, singing "Adore and Be Still", and playing one record, Handel's *Largo*. He signed off wishing his audience (not knowing if he had one) a Merry Christmas and asked that if anyone had heard him, to get in touch about the quality of broadcast. Sparks on ships from hundreds of miles away wrote to him of its success – and a little crackling is always expected at Christmas.

There were further breakthroughs in radio after World War I, but development was slow. In the UK, it was 1920s Chelmsford that hosted the first broadcast, with a performance by Dame Nellie Melba, the Australian soprano and namesake of peach dessert. A consortium of interested parties (interested in radio, not desserts) formed the British Broadcasting Company in 1922.

THE BRITISH BROADCASTING CHRISTMAS

On Christmas Eve 1922, the brand new BBC transmitted the first original British radio drama to London, Birmingham, and Manchester: *The Truth About Father Christmas*, a children's play by Phyllis Twigg. Starring as Father Christmas was Arthur Burrows, "Uncle Arthur" to his listeners, who earlier that year had become Britain's first newsreader. It was a year of firsts, with the Christmas schedule also featuring the first religious broadcast in Reverend John Mayo's Christmas message:

I have come from my church in Whitechapel situated amidst all the noise and the turmoil and the dust and the slums – all that Whitechapel connotes; and it is my privilege through the wizardry of Mr Marconi to speak, as I understand, to many thousands of people. Surely, no man has ever proclaimed the Gospel from such an extraordinary pulpit as I am now doing.

At the time, Reverend Mayo probably held the distinction of preaching to more people than anyone else in history, though radio only reached pockets of the UK at this stage. His hope was that this new medium could continue the legacy of Dickens. The poor and lonely were now invited to the party, with a playlist of carols and a live burst of Schubert from some musicians in the corner of the studio.

The broadcasts continued through Christmas week, including a live New Year's Eve programme complete with "Auld Lang Syne" and a live bagpiper. Until this point the studio had been operating as "London 2LO", in conjunction with the British Broadcasting Company but not fully operated by it. As midnight struck and the piper played, the studio fell under full jurisdiction of the BBC, which currently had 30,000 listeners but just four employees. With 1923, a new era of broadcasting was ushered in, under the stewardship of General Manager (soon to be Director General) John Reith.

The *Illustrated London News* reported that "the invention of broadcasting has immensely extended the power of music to diffuse the spirit of Christmas. The range of carol-singers' voices, hitherto restricted to the limits of a building, a short distance in the open air, has been increased by hundreds of miles."

Not just hundreds, but tens of thousands of miles could now be crossed almost instantly. Yet the new technology needed to be sold. As with the early Christmas cards, supply was not enough – demand had to follow.

Four things Christmas wouldn't be Christmas without...

✧ *PRESENTS…* according to the first line of the book *Little Women*.

- ✧ JOHN MCCLANE… according to a straw poll of my friends, the film *Die Hard* being the favourite choice. Runners-up included sherry, Christmas socks, pigs in blankets, Toblerone, and Dad's strange alcoholic coffee.

- ✧ MARKS & SPENCER… according to the marketing campaign of, oh, British department store Marks & Spencer. Sure enough, Christmas without M&S would be "Chrita" – and that sounds rubbish.

- ✧ THE DOUBLE ISSUE OF THE RADIO TIMES *LISTINGS MAG*… according to me as a child. How else are you going to know when *Die Hard*'s on?

"THE FIRST WIRELESS CHRISTMAS"

The first Christmas *Radio Times* was published on 21 December 1923, three months into the magazine's run, and had its first colour cover. Like the first Christmas card, it featured a simple family Christmas, this time gathered around a fire – but instead facing their new radio receiver. If ever an image summed up our turning away from the flames of Yule logs and Candlemas, the *Radio Times* "Christmas number" had it.

The cover's tagline, "Just a song at twilight", was indicative of the brief schedule, airing on Christmas Day from 6:30 p.m. till midnight. It commenced with *The Children's Hour*, and another Christmas play presented by returning radio Reverend John Mayo. The evening offered music from the London Wireless Orchestra, the Savoy Orpheans, and the Savoy Havana Band, as well as a message on "Wit and Humour" by Reverend G. W. Kerr. The New Year broadcast was the first time that Big Ben's chimes were heard outside of London.

The presence of this in one's own home was still incredibly

novel, to the point that this first Christmas issue included an article by Lord Riddell entitled "Modern Witchcraft". BBC founding father John Reith wrote the magazine's lead article in defence of broadcasting, suggesting benefits such as the opportunity for all to "delight in 'Hunt-the-Slipper' or 'Hunt-the-Thimble' to musical accompaniment – and no one out of the fun at the piano!"

After last year's muted start, Reith declared this "the first wireless Christmas", now that Cardiff, Glasgow, Aberdeen, Bournemouth, and Sheffield had been added to the listenership. Reith especially sought to encourage those who were sceptical: "The loud-speaker is such a convenient entertainer. He is so ready to oblige when wanted, so unassuming when other sport is forward. He doesn't feel hurt if a cracker is pulled in the middle of a song, or offended if the fun grows riotous during his performance."

Yes, one of the original selling-points of radio was that you can switch it off. Sometimes perhaps we forget that today's television has an off button, as it blares out long after we've finished watching what we'd planned.

The very existence of the *Radio Times* shows that broadcasting's early days weren't plain sailing; newspapers refused to print the schedules for fear that radio would see off the printed press. News bulletins were only legally permitted after 7 p.m. each day, to give newspapers the edge.

Like the Dickensian Christmas, radio was a leveller, uniting rich and poor and all corners of the country, even the empire. It was a cultured guest at any Christmas party – though it was the same guest wherever it was heard, and it was a Londoner. That same standardized Christmas was transmitted across the globe from 1932 thanks to the BBC Empire Service, forerunner of the World Service.

It meant that local customs, having survived centuries, were gently being nudged towards the door by the new box in the corner.

That traditional wassail or regular game of "Panic Post" (running around the room to find the right postbox for your letter) resisted a while, but the radio and then the television slowly homogenized the British Christmas. Quirks were pushed to the fringes, as local variations gave way to the capital's Christmas, which became more or less the same as the British Christmas, which became more or less the same as the international Christmas, at least in British outposts across the world.

BETHLEHEM IN CORNWALL

Not everything was London-based. One corner of local culture on the early schedules sprang from a Cornish church. Not far from Truro's original Lessons and Carols service was the parish of St Hilary, home to Reverend Bernard Walke and his self-penned Nativity play. Walke was an unusual priest, who wore a sombrero-like hat and colourful socks and led open-air Sunday services. He was ultimately expelled from his job for violating communion rules, but kept practising anyway until angry coachloads of protestors turned up and ransacked his church.

Before that controversy, he produced his popular Christmas play *Bethlehem* each year. It took some coaxing from BBC producer Filson Young for Walke to loan it for wider broadcast, but Walke relented and *Bethlehem* became Britain's first radio drama broadcast from outside BBC studios. So loved was it, that it became a fixture of BBC Christmas schedules for a decade. It harked back to the medieval mystery plays, and like the Franciscan Nativity cave seven centuries earlier, listeners could imagine they were there at the original scene. Only this time, they didn't need to go to an Italian hill or even a near reconstruction in a Cornish field – it was brought to their living room.

RADIO: THE NOT-ROYAL OPERA HOUSE

American radio transmitted music since the early 1920s, with opera especially popular. On Christmas Day 1931, NBC broadcast a complete opera for the first time on radio: the Metropolitan Opera's *Hansel and Gretel* by Englebert Humperdinck (not that one... the pop star took his name from the nineteenth-century German composer).

In Britain and America, there were safe retellings of familiar productions: classical works, Nativity plays, and countless productions of *A Christmas Carol*. Plays for children and evening music for domestic dancing shaped early broadcasting on both sides of the Atlantic.

King George V certainly felt that this new medium suited these simpler distractions – it was no place for the voice of the crown. In 1923, John Reith tried to convince his king that a rousing royal message from the corner of each living room would inspire the nation. George refused; the monarchy was there to uphold traditions, not start new ones.

A decade later though, the BBC had grown. Reith was no longer General Manager of the national British Broadcasting Company, but Director General of the international British Broadcasting Corporation. Listenership had grown from a handful of cities across Britain to reach the far corners of the empire. George V had lost the chance to give the first royal festive message – Queen Wilhelmina of the Netherlands transmitted to Dutch outposts in Christmas 1931.

The king relented after persistent requests from Reith, a free radio set to try it out for himself, a visit to the BBC studios, and strong encouragement from Queen Mary and the Prime Minister. Radio had shown it was no passing fad. Besides, with the empire now becoming a Commonwealth of equal partners, a message of unity was more important than ever. Within a few years, the platform would become even more crucial as war years again loomed.

On our eleventh date of Christmas…
(Norfolk, 25 December 1932)

In a boxroom under a staircase in Sandringham House, a makeshift radio studio has been created, linking Norfolk's royal rural retreat to London's Broadcasting House. Never has this technology had so lofty a broadcaster; the two large microphones are encased in fine walnut and there is a thick tablecloth – though, whisper it, this has more to do with muffling the king's nervous hands.

King George has been pacing for some hours, unable to enjoy his Christmas Day. He is convinced that this 250-word message is a one-time deal. His principal concern is that when his voice crosses the thresholds of 20 million listeners, it will also cross a line – the sovereign should not be over-familiar. The newspapers have trailed for some time that this will not be a formal address, but a personal greeting – and it will be live. It's not the king's first time on the radio – some of his speeches have been broadcast – but for many this will be their first time hearing a monarch's voice.

George enters the room just before 3 p.m., though the clock reads 3:30, "Sandringham time" – a punctual king, George has all his clocks wound half an hour ahead. In his hand is the script, written for him by Rudyard Kipling. The author of The Jungle Book *and* Just So Stories *was the suggestion of Prime Minister Ramsay MacDonald: an acclaimed writer to ease the king's nerves. The broadcast has been scheduled at the optimal time to reach most parts of the empire during daytime hours – and should coincide with the end of Christmas lunch in many homes.*

As the king sits in a favourite wicker chair, the seat collapses under him. "God bless my soul!" he mutters, his first words in front of the microphone. Before his cue, there is a broadcast introduction from shepherd Walton Handy accompanied by choir-singing and bell-ringing, to bring the British Christmas to Africa, India, Canada, and Australia, as well as throughout the British Isles. Then the king speaks:

> "Through one of the marvels of modern science, I am enabled, this Christmas Day, to speak to all my peoples throughout the empire… I speak now from my home and from my heart to you all. To men and women so cut off by the snows, the deserts, or the seas, that only voices out of the air can reach them; to those cut off from fuller life by blindness, sickness, or infirmity; and to those who are celebrating this day with their children and their grandchildren; to all, to each, I wish a happy Christmas. God bless you…"

FROM GRANDPA ENGLAND TO ONE-TAKE WINDSOR

The response was staggering; the king's authoritative voice earned him the nickname "Grandpa England". Still it was intended to be a one-off; the Prime Minister had to work hard to coax his star into a repeat booking. In January 1933, MacDonald appealed to King George's sense of history, noting how unfortunate it was that Queen Elizabeth's speeches had gone unrecorded. "Damn Queen Elizabeth!" replied the king. After some convincing (and possibly another free radio set or studio tour), George agreed to the encore.

New radio landmarks of Christmas 1933 included the broadcast of bells from Bethlehem, and a popular programme titled *All the World Over*, subsequently renamed *Absent Friends* then *Empire Exchange*, which shared Christmas greetings from across the British empire. New Zealand would hand over to India, who would greet South Africa, and so on.

Twelve more messages from the monarch...

✧   1935… George V's fourth and final festive speech reassured a nation still suffering in the Great Depression, continuing to promote the nostalgic British Christmas.

✧   1936… was speechless, because Edward VIII abdicated just before Christmas.

✧   1937… Edward's brother George VI had a legendary stammer, famously depicted by Colin Firth in *The King's Speech*. Completing his first Christmas message only increased the warmth of the public towards him. In it, he claimed to be unable to match his father's broadcasting skill, but his message of hope against the "shadows of enmity and of fear" was well-received in a fragile world.

✧   1939… After no speech in 1938 came a vital wartime broadcast. Princess Elizabeth suggested that her father quote from the poem "God Knows" by Minnie Louise Haskins:

"And I said to the man who stood at the Gate of the Year,
'Give me a light that I may tread safely into the unknown.'
And he replied,
'Go out into the darkness, and put your hand into the Hand of God.
That shall be to you better than light, and safer than a known way.'"

✧ 1952… Princess became Queen, and Elizabeth II became the third British monarch on the festive airwaves, broadcasting from the same chair and desk as her father and grandfather before her.

✧ 1957… saw the first televised message: "It's inevitable that I should seem a rather remote figure to many of you… but now at least for a few minutes, I welcome you to the peace of my own home." Like the first radio broadcast, Elizabeth assured her audience that timeless values mattered more than new technology. There was an amusing crossed signal too; over the Queen's words, an American police officer was heard to mutter, "Joe, I'm gonna grab a quick coffee."

✧ 1959… had the first pre-recorded message, to be shipped abroad in advance. Wherever you were in the world, you could now hear the message at an appropriate time on Christmas Day.

✧ 1969… had no speech due to fears of oversaturation, after a year of royal documentaries and ceremonies. It was reinstated in 1970; the public loved the royal broadcaster, as did the technicians, who nicknamed Her Majesty "One-Take Windsor".

✧ 1992… The sixtieth anniversary of the royal message was Elizabeth's self-professed "annus horribilis": two of her sons' marriages ended, Windsor Castle suffered a fire, and tabloid interest in the royal family reached new highs (or lows). As if to prove the point, *The Sun* newspaper published a leaked version of the speech two days early. For the previous five years, naturalist and broadcaster David Attenborough had produced the speech; maybe he should have stayed on.

✧   1997… was the first speech broadcast online.

✧   2006… was the first royal Christmas podcast.

✧   2012… was shot in 3D – without the customary reassurance that timeless values matter more than new technology. A version in Smell-O-Vision has yet to appear.

THE MODERN ROYAL CHRISTMAS

The new Elizabethan age welcomed a softening of the hierarchical Christmases of the past – no mouth-dabbing servants, castle-shaped salt cellars, or farting jesters here.

At a typical British royal Christmas, the extended family gather at Sandringham House, arriving in order of inferiority: junior royals first on 23 December, the heir to the throne joining later the next day. The youngest royals decorate the tree under supervision from the monarch, followed by German-style Christmas Eve present-opening and a formal supper.

Christmas morning sees the customary royal walk to church, possibly harking back to the Holy Days and Fasting Days Act of 1551, which states that every citizen must attend church on Christmas Day, without using any kind of vehicle. The Act was repealed in 1969, though perhaps no one ever told the Queen. Her Majesty's church-bound perambulation has made Christmas Day headlines throughout her reign, almost as a trailer for her three o'clock message.

Before that though, lunch: Christmas turkey with all the trimmings, but no hams – and no young children. Their place is in the nursery, dining under supervision from Nanny. After a walk around the estate, the royal gathering watch the pre-recorded speech live, apart from the one who gave it, who watches in a separate room – it's never nice watching oneself.

Still hungry? There's afternoon tea of Yule log and Christmas cake, while supper is a free-for-all buffet to allow the staff some time off. One favourite platter was a whole Stilton cheese, pitchforked on top with port poured on to seep through. They say it's rather nice on a cracker, though surely you'll dampen the bang and get a soggy crown. Then again, they've got enough crowns lying around.

All that banqueting uses over 1,000 glasses and can require three weeks' worth of washing-up and cleaning. Looks like there's still a place for some seasonal regal pomp.

Down the pecking order in family homes across the country, domestic refrigeration arrived post-war. That ancient Norse problem of icy food storage came full circle, helping us load up for the season. The shops seized on our new space, so Christmas party food became big business. For those who didn't fancy cooking the full banquet, Marks & Spencer offered Christmas ready meals from as early as 1958.

Defrosted lunch being digested, the three o'clock custom of watching the royal message has endured, especially amongst older family members. Younger Brits might prefer Channel 4's *Alternative Christmas Message*, by Sharon Osborne or The Simpsons.

Christmas has proven to be primetime for advertising the monarchy to the world. While British broadcasting was busy selling Merrie Old – or Merry New – England via radio, royals, and carols, America ploughed the furrow of fiction. From music to movies, seasonal sentiment embedded itself in the American Christmas – and as in Britain, these new seeds of tradition grew on the battlefields.

Bing Crosby, Rosemary Clooney, Vera Ellen and Danny Kaye, in the 1954 Paramount production of *White Christmas*

Chapter 12

Bing to Bublé

(1934–PRESENT)

In the Roaring Twenties, Christmases Lindy-Hopped and Charlestoned towards the extravagant – but the partying was muted by the Turbulent Thirties. In the grip of the Great Depression, festivities became a checklist of traditions, to be observed, checked off, and rarely added to. Trees went up, stockings were hung, and basic presents were given. North America clung to links to its past, regardless of whether they were Germanic, English, or its own home-grown customs.

Innovative technology created music and movie industries – so the festive season's new guests were in popular culture. One of the earliest Christmas hits, 1934's "Winter Wonderland", was written in West Mountain Sanitarium, where Dick Smith was being treated for tuberculosis, with a view of frosty fields. The same year, Santa gained a new soundtrack with the radio launch of "Santa Claus is Coming to Town", three years into the figure's campaign for Coke. It became an instant hit, and scholars still debate whether the definitive version is by Frank Sinatra, The Jackson 5, Bruce Springsteen, or Alvin and the Chipmunks.

In this chapter, we'll chart the Christmas songs that spanned the twentieth century, and we'll enjoy some seasonal spectaculars on the big and small screens.

RUDOLPH THE RED-NOSED RATINGS-WINNER

The Great Depression massively affected Christmas spending. Novel approaches were needed to usher in customers, so throughout the 1930s the Chicago department store Montgomery Ward bought in colouring books to give away to children – but to keep costs down they asked their in-house advertising copywriter to make one for them, a happy animal story. Copywriter Robert L. May drew inspiration from his four-year-old daughter Barbara's much-loved trips to the zoo, where she particularly enjoyed the deer.

As he wrote verses of this new poem, he read them to her, for her approval. They tried several different names for the lead reindeer character – Rollo and Reginald were rejected before landing on Rudolph.

Like Clement Clarke Moore's Santa story a century earlier, the first audience for the finished poem was the writer's immediate family: his daughter and his in-laws. May's wife sadly died from cancer in the summer of 1939, before the book was finished. His boss offered to remove him from the project, but May threw himself into it, finishing it just a month after losing his wife.

Two and a half million copies were distributed that Christmas, to unprecedented success. A reprint was delayed for another seven years due to wartime rationing (presumably you can turn reindeer colouring books into bombs), but when paper stocks allowed, another 3 and a half million copies were handed out to Montgomery Ward customers. The copyright was held by the store until the late forties, when the store's president graciously, generously, possibly foolishly handed the rights to the author free of charge.

May's brother-in-law Johnny Marks put music to the words in 1949, creating not just "Rudolph the Red-Nosed Reindeer", but a career in Christmas song composition, under his own St Nicholas Music publishing company. He went on to write over twenty Christmas songs, including hits like "Run Rudolph Run", "A Holly Jolly Christmas", and "Rockin' Around the Christmas Tree".

Rudolph led the pack and suddenly lots more festive belters followed. The original "Rudolph the Red-Nosed Reindeer" was offered to Bing Crosby, who turned it down – so "The Singing Cowboy" Gene Autry stepped in to make their reindeer song famous. When Autry cottoned on to the success of Christmas character songs, he followed up with "Here Comes Santa Claus" and a new creation, "Frosty the Snowman". "Rudolph" was always out in front though, still the world's second-best-selling Christmas song until the 1980s – in all that time only beaten by Bing himself.

Because no one beats Bing. Back when Rudolph was only a colouring book awaiting a wartime reprint, Bing was debuting not just the world's most popular Christmas song, but what would become the best-selling song of all time.

THE WORLD'S NUMBER ONE

The attack on Pearl Harbor pulled the United States into World War II in early December 1941. Two weeks later on Christmas Eve, Churchill and Roosevelt united in Washington for a sombre lighting of the White House tree, the final such ceremony for three years due to energy restrictions.

Japanese aggression meant that in Hong Kong, this would be known as "Black Christmas". The day after that White House Christmas, the world was given a much-needed dose of sentimental nostalgia in melodic form: "White Christmas".

On our twelfth date of Christmas…
(Los Angeles, 25 December 1941)
The world needs a pick-me-up, and Bing thinks he has it. He's chosen to launch his song on the Christmas Day edition of his own radio hour, NBC's Kraft Music Hall. The show is especially popular with young men, many of whom will be spending one last Christmas with their families before being shipped out to war.

Bing's hosted the show since 1936, another string to the bow of the world's biggest star. There are bigger movie stars, but none with eighty hit records and a broadcasting career. No one moves between media with the same ease as Bing.

Already he's sold more records than anyone in the history of recorded music. Seven years ago, he arguably saved the record industry single-handed, when he became the first artist to agree on royalties rather than a flat fee – it kept Decca Records in business and paved the way for the singles industry to come. Recently he was one of the few voices campaigning for Louis Armstrong to receive the same billing as his white co-stars. It all contributes to him being voted "most admired man alive"; by the end of the decade, some radio stations will play half Bing Crosby songs, half non-Bing. His new song today is buried amid nine others, as well as the usual gang-show chitchat and commercials for Kraft food.

Bing can thank these new microphones for taking his career to unprecedented levels. It helped change his singing style from back-of-the-room belting like Al Jolson, to laidback crooning. Bing's trademark easy singing, and easy listening, opens the show with "Adeste Fidelis" ("O Come, All Ye Faithful"), then non-festive favourites like "Chattanooga Choo-Choo" and "Oh! How I Hate to Get Up in the Morning". It's the final show of Bing's regular guest vocalist Connie Boswell, one of a dozen or so in this packed Studio B of Hollywood's Radio City on the corner of Sunset and Vine.

Halfway through the hour, he introduces "White Christmas" and the band strike up. Bing expects a hit, but little more. When the song's writer Irving Berlin brought it to him, Bing thought it was fine enough, telling him, "I don't think we have any problems with that one, Irving."

Inspiration struck Berlin last Christmas – never a time of celebration for him, either from his Russian Jewish upbringing, or here in the States, having lost his three-week-old son on Christmas Day 1928. Last Christmas, the prolific writer was stuck in a California hotel room, penning songs for Bing's new picture Holiday Inn. Irving harked back to his snowy Colorado mountain home, thinking of the family white Christmas that he was missing.

He took the finished song to his musical secretary for notation – Berlin composed one song a day, yet couldn't write music. "I just wrote the best song I've ever written," he said. "Heck, I just wrote the best song that anybody's ever written."

As America hears it for the first time, millions experience those same pangs felt by Berlin as he wrote it. Wistfulness, peace, and nostalgia come through in the eight simple sentences. It will take till next Christmas, when Armed Forces Radio take the song across the world, for it to reach classic status, as a reminder of home.

The Christmas 1941 broadcast ends with Bing reprising "Silent Night", his first Christmas hit from 1935 and the current best-selling single of all-time – until this new song tops it. Those who miss the broadcast will never get to hear this unique version; the song's recording for release will be made the following springtime, and the 1941 broadcast lost.

HOME FOR CHRISTMAS... AND AWAY

Months later, Bing recorded the song in just eighteen minutes – but even that isn't the version we know today. The 1942 recording became so overplayed that it was too damaged for future use. The familiar version echoing through shopping centres each December (and November, and October) is a 1947 re-recording; Bing reunited his band to accurately recreate their 1942 session.

The song sold over 50 million copies worldwide, a figure unlikely to ever be matched. Its use in the festive classic movie *Holiday Inn* won Irving Berlin an Oscar – the only person ever to open the envelope, read his own name, and hand the award to himself. A movie sequel, *White Christmas*, is now the most repeated film on TV each Christmas – even though *Holiday Inn* is the original and arguably the best (and I will have that argument any time).

Crosby carried the song – and the American wistful Christmas – all over world as he visited troops, though he was reluctant to sing it for fear of upsetting the soldiers so far from home. It was still requested at every stop, even in the height of summer, and Bing always obliged. When he realized how homesickness could keep the troops going, Bing added "I'll Be Home for Christmas" to his festive canon in 1943, with its bittersweet twist that the singer is only home in his dreams.

"White Christmas" had a significant role in a later war, serving as the warning alarm to leave Saigon in April 1975. Operation Frequent Wind's evacuation plan was triggered when American Forces Radio broadcast the code: "The temperature in Saigon is 105 degrees and rising", followed by Bing's song. The jolt of hearing a Christmas classic in sweltering Saigon urged thousands to the helicopters. The song had transported US troops home in their minds thirty years previously, and now it brought 1,000 Americans home, 6,000 Vietnamese out of Saigon, and the Vietnam War to a close.

Through war and peace, Bing's legacy was to create a cultural industry around Christmas, out-Dickensing even Dickens in terms of winter nostalgia. Family, simplicity, and snow were now inseparable parts of a festival that for centuries had not been family-oriented, had been anything but simple, and had sunny origins in the Middle East and Mediterranean – where the treetops rarely glistened.

Five Christmas crooners...

✧ *"HAVE YOURSELF A MERRY LITTLE CHRISTMAS"*...
Homely wartime reminders continued with Judy Garland's
performance in the 1944 movie *Meet Me in St. Louis*.
Garland's character reassures her five-year-old sister
with a message of optimism, though its lyrics have been
changed over the years. The unfilmed original suggested
that this may be the listener's last Christmas, till the
lyrics were changed to cheerier talk of lightness of heart.
Frank Sinatra's cover version altered it further, with less
muddling through and more hanging up of stars. The
unrecorded original suggested we'd be together if the Lord
allows, though the film's producers preferred a secular
version – so the fates now do the allowing.

✧ *"BABY, IT'S COLD OUTSIDE"*... 1944's duet, dodgy
sexual politics 'n' all, began as a party piece by Frank
Loesser and his wife Lynn Garland, to tell guests it's
time to leave. When Frank sold the song to MGM, Lynn
fumed as it was "their song". A genuine marital row – how
Christmassy.

✧ *"THE CHRISTMAS SONG"*... Allegedly the world's most
performed Christmas song, written in the sweltering
summer of 1945. Sick of roasting in the open sun, lyricist
Bob Wells wrote four wintry lines about chestnuts and
carols. Jack Frost and co were intended to take his mind
off the heat. His collaborator and noted jazz singer Mel
Tormé saw the scribblings and forty minutes later they
had their song. After the original recording, Nat King
Cole knew he could improve on his first rendition, so
insisted on a new version, with its now well-known string

arrangement. Shame about the ageist lyrics – excluding a Merry Christmas for anyone below the age of one or over the age of ninety-two. Tut tut.

✧ *"LET IT SNOW! LET IT SNOW! LET IT SNOW!"*… The same hot summer as "The Christmas Song's" overcooked genesis, this snowy favourite was being written just around the corner.

✧ *"SLEIGH RIDE"*… was written in the sweltering summer of 1946 – yet another musical distraction. Nothing gets you in the Christmas spirit like a Hollywood heatwave.

THE NUTCRACKER – SWEET

The post-war era brought a desire to dig deep into tradition, and Christmas was the perfect time to do just that. American history brought several holiday customs to mind, from Santa hats to eggnog, but old Europe managed to export some of its cultural wares too. The 1914 Ukrainian "Carol of the Bells" embedded itself as an American favourite – originally written as a folk song for spring, but given new Christmas lyrics on arrival in the United States. Americans similarly adopted a full Russian ballet, underappreciated back home.

On 24 December 1944, the San Francisco Ballet gave the first complete performance of Tchaikovsky's *The Nutcracker*, to such positive reviews that they've repeated the performance every Christmas Eve since. The New York City Ballet gave what for many was the definitive performance in 1954, and by the sixties the piece had become a national Christmas institution. Since then, around half of North American ballet ticket sales each year are for *The Nutcracker* – though its success was far from assured until this point.

In 1816, Ernst Hoffman came up with the macabre story of toys coming to life on Christmas Eve. The tale of broken jaws, fevered dreams, and mouse children dying in mousetraps was adapted by Alexandre Dumas (author of *The Three Musketeers* and *The Count of Monte Cristo*), forming the basis of Tchaikovsky's ballet. After its St Petersburg debut in Christmas 1892, the critics were not kind: the original Sugar Plum Fairy was reviewed as "podgy", while the adaptation itself was thought to be unfaithful to Hoffman's original. The use of children in the cast was probably a mistake too, so new touring versions in the 1930s corrected this with an all-adult cast. By the time it reached the United States, the ballet had been a fifty-year work-in-progress, and was finally ready to become a Christmas classic.

Perhaps the most-loved element is the music box sound of what was then a new instrument called the celesta. Tchaikovsky heard the new invention played in Paris while writing the music, so he begged his publishers to buy one in. They had to keep it a secret from rival composers like Rimsky-Korsakov though, so that Tchaikovsky could be the first to showcase the twinkly wonder.

The ballet still makes headlines today. In January 2017, a Siberian archbishop denounced *The Nutcracker* as a "work of the occult" featuring a "prince shape-shifter" – but then again he was pushing a new Christmas opera written by the wife of a local priest, scheduled alongside it. Between the sacred and the secular, the grand war of the arts rumbles on.

Eleven generous Christmas uncles – who gave us at least TWO big gifts! Some Thank You notes...

✧ *Dear St Francis of Assisi,* Thanks for the live Nativity scenes and for carols that weren't Latin.

✧ *Dear Martin Luther,* I've nailed this letter to your door to say thanks for helping St Nick turn into Santa with all your reforming. Mummy says you gave us the Christmas tree too but I'm not sure.

✧ *Dear Oliver Cromwell,* Thank you for making mince pies round, and for making us like Father Christmas more because he was nice compared to you. You made the first proper defenders of Christmas, which is a bit like people nowadays wondering if they'll call Christmas "Winterval" but not really.

✧ *Dear Washington Irving,* Thanks for Santa and for making the cold English Christmas sound quite nice really.

✧ *Dear Prince Albert,* Thank you for the tree and for all German things like gingerbread and German markets and stollen bread though Mummy says you shouldn't steal things.

✧ *Dear Sir Henry Cole,* Thank you for all the Christmas cards and for making the museums and the Albert Hall for me to visit for Christmas concerts – we had a lovely time.

✧ *Dear Tom Smith,* Thank you for the crackers and paper decorations, your jokes aren't funny.

✧ *Dear Charles Dickens,* Thanks very much for snow and Scrooge and charity and mulled wine.

✧   *Dear Rowland Macy,* Thank you for the in-store Santa and the window displays and the cash refunds in January when I don't like my presents.

✧   *Dear Bishop Benson,* Thanks for Nine Lessons and Carols and for the Christmas ghost story.

✧   *Dear Bing Crosby,* Thanks for the Christmas single and bucketloads of nostalgia. Thanks too for ploughing your not inconsiderable wealth into developing technology like VHS videotapes. I don't know what they are but Mummy says it meant she could watch *Home Alone* and *The Snowman* in the nineties.

GOING TO THE PICTURES

As peacetime resumed, incomes improved and family Christmases swelled. Presents and turkeys enlarged, and seasonal theatre trips came back into fashion – but with fresh competition, from the box office and the box in the corner. Whether cinema outing or home viewing, the family preference was for good, clean, high-quality fun. Films like *The Wizard of Oz*, *The Sound of Music*, and *The Great Escape* became inextricably linked to the season, even though witchy tornados, escaping the Nazis, and escaping the Nazis aren't exactly Christmassy.

Frank Capra's *It's a Wonderful Life* began life as a short story in 1939 – writer Philip Van Doren Stern struggled to publish it so turned it into a Christmas card, which handily ended up on the desk of a Hollywood producer. The movie made a loss on its 1947 release, and like those other favourites, it took another two or three decades to become a fixture of Christmas TV schedules.

One innovation from Capra's film was a new snow effect. Till now, movie snow largely had been comprised of cornflakes painted white, which was a little crunchy underfoot, so Capra instead threw 27,000 litres of a soapy foamite substance at a wind machine. Fake snow became big business at homes across the Western world, especially since Bing's "White Christmas" popularized the idea when there was little snowfall to be seen. Unfortunately a lot of the early mixtures were made from rather lethal asbestos.

Six months later, another Christmas classic hit the silver screen: *Miracle on 34th Street*. It had an unusual May theatrical release, since the studio doubted that Christmas would yield much box office. To lure summer moviegoers in, the original posters and trailer hid all the festive elements – even though the entire plot concerns one Kris Kringle claiming to be the real Santa.

From this 1947 gem to *Jingle All the Way*, American cinema has done the "Christmas shopping" film far better than Britain, because the consumer Christmas is their baby. When Britain tries it… well 1954's *The Crowded Day* wasn't memorable. That said, not all American movies about Santa Claus are sure-fire hits. The Internet Movie Database "Bottom 100" is littered with Santa movies, from 1964's *Santa Claus Conquers the Martians* to the Hulk Hogan vehicle *Santa with Muscles*.

GHOSTS AND GREMLINS

The American film industry may do commercialism well, but the British film industry sticks to what it knows – the past. So that's plenty of ghost stories like *The Woman in White* or *The Turn of the Screw*, though our favourite ghosts have remained those that haunted Ebenezer Scrooge.

The first screen adaptation of *A Christmas Carol* appeared just a generation after Dickens' death. Early versions often began with a book being removed from a shelf, to again forge that link with past entertainment. The styles vary – from Alastair Sim's definitive 1951 *Scrooge* to Kermit's Bob Cratchit in *The Muppet Christmas Carol* – but the story speaks to new generations.

Bill Murray updated Victorian miserliness to modern cynicism in *Scrooged*, and the same year another TV comic actor broke through (he broke a lot of things) in 1988's *Die Hard*. It's one of the odder choices for a Christmas film, but to this day there are annual Advent viewings of John McClane's festive nightmare. By now, Christmas movies had a dark streak, whether in the comedy horror of *Gremlins*, the fantasy insanity of *The Nightmare Before Christmas*, or the jet-black worldview of *Bad Santa* – though that film shared Christmas 2003 receipts with brighter fare like *Elf* and *Love Actually*, so we're clearly not all cynics.

RETURN OF THE YULE LOG: NOW IN 2D

By far the bigger festive viewing figures are to be found in front of the smaller screen – which nowadays can be very small indeed, as families watch different shows on different devices. Before tablets and phones changed viewing habits, the golden age of Christmas telly gave us half a century of classics to unite the family – even if we weren't talking to each other.

In the United States, that often meant animation. Sixties favourites like Charlie Brown or *The Grinch Who Stole Christmas* were repeated *ad infinitum*, as parents tried to give their children the same Christmas they had enjoyed. They could even recreate the log fires of their youth, without needing a fireplace, thanks to TV exec Fred Thrower's quirky idea.

In 1966, Thrower decided to "warm up" a few homes, as well as give his station staff some time off, by filming a log burning in the New York mayor's fireplace. He then broadcast it on a loop for two hours, costing 4,000 dollars in lost advertising revenue. It became an annual hit running for twenty-four consecutive Christmases.

Today the YouTube equivalents still garner millions of views, as we pretend our Yule log is burning away just as it did for centuries. Except rather than burn for twelve straight days, Thrower's version burned for just seventeen seconds before looping around again.

THIS TIME NEXT YEAR...

In Britain, the comedy special has been the staple diet of our post-turkey TV feast. Must-watch comedians of the day scored unsurpassable viewing figures, like 1977's specials from Mike Yarwood (with the highest viewing figures for any Christmas Day show at 21.4 million) and Morecambe & Wise (a still very respectable 21.3 million). As a comedy writer myself, I spent the build-up to Christmas 2016 writing... an ITV retrospective on Morecambe & Wise, revisiting all the right sketches, just not necessarily in the right order. For Britain's largest single TV audience of all time, see *Only Fools and Horses'* 1996 Christmas special – 24.35 million people watched Del Boy and Rodney finally become millionaires.

Elsewhere on the schedules, a modern-day British Christmas wouldn't be complete without Raymond Briggs' heart-warming *The Snowman*, a *Top of the Pops* recap of the year, and a timely reminder from *EastEnders* that our family Christmas isn't as bad as it can get. Their 1986 special was the most-watched TV show of all time (over two viewings – so *Only Fools* trumps it for the at-the-time audience).

JUMPERS AND JEDI

The night before Britain's record-breaking contributions from Yarwood and Morecambe & Wise, ITV broadcast Bing Crosby's final offering on Christmas Eve 1977. Bing died between recording and broadcast, leaving us with *Bing Crosby's Merrie Olde*

Christmas – once again showing that Ye Olde England somehow had first dibs on the seasonal backdrop, even for America's king of Christmas. It was a festive compendium of greatest hits: a log fire, sketches about Dickens, a cover of "Have Yourself a Merry Little Christmas", "Jingle Bells" from a children's choir, and most famously a bemused duet with newcomer David Bowie. This was not like the ones Bing used to know.

These seasonal specials had become American TV staples, with fireside crooning from singer-presenters like Andy Williams and Val Doonican. We have them to thank too for a festive fashion monstrosity: the Christmas jumper. Garish sweaters were a handy way of showing lounge-suited entertainers at rest, their cosy downtime with a convenient film crew on hand to pick up every impromptu quip and ditty. So like your dad trying too hard to dress down from his work suit, the Christmas sweater became an embarrassment. Kitsch comes full circle though, so at the time of writing, the Christmas jumper is back. Which means by the time of reading, it'll probably be gone again.

The variety special was never better sent up than in *Knowing Me, Knowing Yule with Alan Partridge*, broadcast live from a replica of Alan's Norwich house – surely a modern Bracebridge Hall. For the format at its worst, see 1978's *Star Wars Holiday Special*. Never-repeated lowlights include: *Dynasty*'s Diahann Carroll performing an erotic fantasy song for Chewbacca's dad Itchy, cameoing comedians propping up the Cantina bar, and Princess Leia's musical finale adding Wookiee "Life Day" lyrics to the *Star Wars* theme. This, not *The Empire Strikes Back*, was technically the first *Star Wars* sequel, though George Lucas said of this hopeless Jedi menace, "if I had the time and a sledgehammer, I would track down every copy of that show and smash it." Bad luck, George – even if you attacked all the clones, the Internet has awakened.

The force may have been weak with this sci-fi (un-)spectacular, but Harrison Ford looked no more bewildered than Bing Crosby a year earlier in that David Bowie duet. Yet they mustered magic in a way that Wookiee warbling never would. When Bowie's prayerful "Peace on Earth" interlaced with Crosby's "Little Drummer Boy", the old guard effectively handed over the keys of Christmas, then moved on to the manor house in the sky.

"Little Drummer Boy" was a decades-old song, made famous by The Harry Simeone Chorale; their follow-up "Do You Hear What I Hear?", actually a protest song against the Cuban Missile Crisis, reflected Christmas music's changing political flavour. As in Bowie's hopeful counterpoint to Bing's carol, festive pop culture was becoming less about yearning for the past, and more about pleading for the present and future.

Ten stories behind The Best Christmas Album in the Universe (well, pop at least), ever...

✧   *"STOP THE CAVALRY"*… Not a Christmas song but a protest song that mentions Christmas. When Lewie utters that "Chrrristmas", it makes me wonder if there's something about the sound of the word itself. If swear words are satisfying because of the hard consonants, then by the same logic, the hard "C" of "Christmas" flows into the softer "s"s, the hard year giving way to an extended gentler, more cushioning time. Go on, say it, pause between the "Ch" and the "r". Am I mad?

✧   *"A CHRISTMAS GIFT FOR YOU"*… Phil Spector's "Wall of Sound" was the one-stop shop for the sixties festive cover version. Christmas number ones that decade were dominated by The Beatles, who topped the UK charts four Christmases out of ten.

✧ *"HAPPY XMAS (WAR IS OVER)"*… John and Yoko's protest was against the Vietnam War, via their post-honeymoon bed-ins – they invited an eager press who thought they'd see some lovin', rather than some love-out. This was the first Christmas song by a Beatle – McCartney's "Wonderful Christmastime" soon followed, with Ringo's "I Wanna Be Santa Claus" much later.

✧ *"MERRY XMAS EVERYBODY"*… Slade saw off Wizzard's "I Wish it Could Be Christmas Everyday" in the glam war of December 1973. Noddy Holder wrote the song to cheer along working-class Brits amid economic gloom, creating Britain's first Christmas-themed Christmas number one.

✧ *"I BELIEVE IN FATHER CHRISTMAS"*… Christmas culture has always borrowed from the past to give to the present: Greg Lake's 1975 hit used Prokofiev's *Lieutenant Kijé*; the same year, Mike Oldfield harked back 650 years for his new version of "In Dulci Jubilo".

✧ *"DO THEY KNOW IT'S CHRISTMAS"*… Political Christmas music reached its zenith with the fastest-selling single in UK history, inspired by Michael Buerk's 1984 news report on the famine in Ethiopia. Bob Geldof roped in Midge Ure, then bumped into Gary Kemp outside an antiques shop and asked him to join, and before you know it, you have a supergroup. Previous Christmas hit-makers like Paul McCartney and David Bowie couldn't make it but sent messages of support that made the B-side. Status Quo were meant to add their voices, but turned up hungover and couldn't reach the high notes. Others, like Marilyn – and even Nigel Planer from *The Young Ones* – weren't invited but turned up anyway.

✧ *"DRIVING HOME FOR CHRISTMAS"*… Always the first song I play in my car on my last commute of the year, Chris Rea's lift home from London to Middlesbrough inspired the classic. The demise of the automatically rosy family celebration was reflected in other eighties and nineties hits, from city singletons (The Waitresses' "Christmas Wrapping") to unrequited love (Wham!'s "Last Christmas").

✧ *"MISTLETOE AND WINE"*… The occasional wistful voice of nostalgia, such as Cliff Richard, channelled the ghost of Bing. Cliff's 99th single began life in the musical *The Little Match Girl*: the titular character is kicked into the snow by middle-class baddies and ironically sings of the perfect Christmas she doesn't have.

✧ *"A FAIRYTALE OF NEW YORK"*… The Pogues' booze-raddled break-up rant was the product of a wager with manager Elvis Costello, who bet them that they couldn't write a Christmas song. The much-loved result draws on forties New York (the piano intro was inspired by Ennio Morricone's *Once Upon a Time in America*, my own favourite soundtrack as it goes), again harking back to a golden era that trickles through our hands before we can clutch it.

✧ *"ALL I WANT FOR CHRISTMAS IS YOU"*… Mariah Carey's 1994 megahit is practically a Christmas checklist: part Nutcracker music box, part bouncy reindeer ride, a dose of Motown, a dollop of Garlandesque wailing, a few bells and whistles, all wrapped up in an unrequited Wall of Sound that says forget commercialism, forget the tree, forget the snow (in fact here's a long list of all the things I don't want…), I just want you.

STILL HARKING

Perhaps these festive songs, films, and TV shows have future-proofed Christmas. As long as we keep craving our cultural hit each December, we'll keep on celebrating – and the stores certainly won't let us stop.

It's been sung that we get the Christmas we deserve. Maybe in our postmodern world, we flock to Christmas culture that's as broken as we are – which might be why the Nativity story has stayed well out of popular culture. We love the familiar, whether *A Christmas Carol* or a borrowed classical riff, but we haven't returned much to the manger. We prefer our songs, films, and characters full of imperfection, so the stories we retell are about those who need redemption, rather than a perfect baby who does the redeeming.

All stories are lessons, so the history of Christmas is a service of a Thousand Lessons and Nearly as Many Carols. For 2,000 years we've looked over our shoulder, at that Christmas over there, just out of reach. We continue to wonder if it was better then, and what we can learn, and if maybe in the next twelve months, we can get it right.

Wrapping Up

LAST CHRISTMAS… AND NEXT

If you've made it this far – congratulations. You've earned a sherry and a mince pie, even if you're reading this in July (this makes an unusual summer read, but then *Miracle on 34th Street* made an unusual summer film). If you don't have a mince pie, demand one from your nearest supermarket – they'll be stocking them soon in their countdown to Christmas.

Today may feel swamped with more traditions than you can shake a snow globe at (snow globes! I knew we'd missed out something), but it's the same push-pull game that there's always been – object of the game: ownership of the season. Only now, there are more players. From Bublé to baubles, crackers to cranberry sauce, Jona Lewie to John Lewis – everyone wants a piece of the trillion-dollar industry.

In the crowded musical marketplace, one Christmas hit isn't enough, so our choirs of earth-bound angels layer flavour on festive flavour. Michael Bublé covers Mariah; Kylie somehow duets with Sinatra; the now-baritone Aled Jones oddly duets with his younger soprano self (a performance I hope he'll repeat in another thirty years as a bass). You can't just sing a Christmas song – you have to cover someone else's and drag in another Christmas icon. It's the musical equivalent of the turducken in the kitchen – bird within bird within bird, possibly basted with the juices of a fourth. One day Slade and The Pogues will sing "Do They Know it's Christmas" with Bing Crosby on backing vocals, and Christmas will be complete (it sounds painful, but ripping off a Band Aid always is). As this book hits shelves, Mariah Carey's *All I Want for Christmas is You* hits cinemas: an animated film based entirely on her song lyrics. A scene-per-line adaptation of "Santa Baby", starring a Kardashian, must be just a few film festivals away.

As for commerce, the tills may remain silent on Christmas Day, but Internet sales mean we're shopping contactless, from our sofa, while still digesting the turkey. The Christmas commercial is now a thing to be trailed and hyped like it's a product itself, rather than advertising where to buy them. In Britain, John Lewis has lately won the war of retail advertising, with year upon year of sanguine animal stories, from tobogganing penguins to trampolining Boxer dogs. The commercial is trailed with a release date and you may even have to watch a sponsored ad before the ad. (Sorry – another ad vent.)

Old family days like Stir-Up Sunday have been nudged out, in favour of Black Friday, Cyber Monday, and even Take-back Tuesday. After all, shops didn't earn a penny on Stir-Up Sunday, so in whose interest is it to keep it going? The future of Christmas seems to be dictated by those with the biggest stake in it – the stores.

Customs have only ever thrived when there's demand for them at ground level, and while some shoppers have seized on Black Friday sales, many have shunned them; there are now concerted campaigns to celebrate "Buy Nothing Day" on the same day. Then again, where's the harm in a bit of spending, if it helps pay people's wages, keeps businesses going, and stops a run on the bank *a la* George Bailey in *It's a Wonderful Life*? As long as we can afford it – and don't go spending money we don't have.

The hope is that we still make our own Christmas. We don't *have* to go sales shopping, or retire to different rooms to watch different channels (thanks to our devices, we can now watch different channels in the same room). We don't have to have arguments about whether we should have a real tree or an artificial one (actually in our house, we do have to have that…). Instead we can shape the occasion as we wish. The Internet isn't evil – as well as driving sales, it can bring us closer. One friend of mine plays family board games via Skype each Christmas, so that those overseas can get a look in. Or maybe they're in the next room being Scrooges – I never thought to ask.

And what of the church? Alas a little late to the Christmas party, it took so long to decide whether and how to celebrate it, festive culture has grown around it and can't be cut back. The church still has its Christmas, a constant at the heart of the festivities – the "Silent Night" while the cash tills and Saturnalian party rage around it. Hasn't that always been the case, ever since the quiet crib in a boisterous Roman empire? Fads may come and go, but whether it's St Francis of Assisi's living Nativity or Bishop Benson bringing carols back to church, Christianity keeps telling its story – which is fine, because at Christmas we love a repeat.

Whether church or store, to innovate, history has shown us that you need a balance of tradition and originality – see also Twitter-based Lessons and Carols or Google Maps' Santa Tracker. They say that door-to-door carollers are on the way out (well they never came in), partly thanks to Halloween's trick-or-treaters getting a jump on them, but largely because in-store Christmas soundtracks now start so early that we've had enough of them by December. My idea to unite old and new? The viral wassailing flashmob. Look out for it next year, folks.

I asked some pals for their guesses at where Christmas commerce goes next: Jez thinks it's 3D-printed gifts (you buy the voucher for the bike, your loved one prints it), while Ro expects that Santa drones will drop pressies through kids' windows at a time of your choosing. Rachel's just shown me an app where a pre-recorded Santa phones your child, "chats" about a few of their favourite (pre-entered) things, then sends them to bed. Helen predicts holographic Christmas trees; Jonathan reckons we'll be the holograms around a real tree, family from around the world e-reunited.

The community Christmas remains as important as ever. In an individualistic smartphone existence, local customs get us out looking at lights being switched on or trees going up (or where I'm from, the legendary Windlesham Pram Race – it's a must each Boxing Day). They're also free, which is great for those worried that Christmas is costing us more each year.

For those worried about overspending, perhaps look to the royals, as we did 200 years ago. For Christmas gifts the Royal Family buy each other the naffest present they can find. Restoring the fun to gift-giving does us all a bit of good, and might prevent meltdowns in shopping centres.

One true story tells of two brothers-in-law, Larry Kunkel and Roy Collett. In 1964, Larry's mother bought him some moleskin trousers, which Larry passed on to Roy the next Christmas. But Roy didn't want them either, so the next Christmas after that, he gave them back to Roy. After a few years of alternating ownership and the familiar sight of the trousers wrapped up in a bow under the tree, Roy had an idea. When he had custody of "the Christmas pants", he wrapped them up a little more firmly – in a metal pipe three feet long and just one inch wide. Good luck in getting those out…

Larry did. And when next Christmas came, he handed them back to Roy with wrapping of his own – a ball of almost impenetrable barbed wire. Almost, but not quite. Back and forth they continued, year on year, with escalating challenges to unwrap the darned things. One year they'd be mounted in an insulated window, another they'd be stuffed into a soldered coffee tin then buried in concrete. There was a safe welded shut, a glove compartment of a car crushed into a three-foot cube, and a giant concrete-filled tyre with a cheery note attached reading "Have a Goodyear". Still the trousers were always retrievable and impressively hard-wearing. That is, until Roy accidentally burned them to a crisp pouring four tonnes of molten glass over them. That Christmas, twenty-six years on, Larry received the ashes in an urn. A note attached read, "Sorry old man, here lies the pants."

Tempted as I am to finish a book on the history of Christmas with the word "pants", one final postscript. Some of the stories we've looked at may not be true. I've no idea if St Boniface or Martin Luther ever had woodland walks that inspired the Christmas tree, or whether St Nicholas' bones ever sweated myrrh. But these are the stories that have been retold through the centuries, that have shaped our Christmas. As a story fan and a Christmas nut, it's been a joy to get to know these tales, even if I did get some odd looks in the library researching this in August.

Writers like Joseph Campbell and Christopher Vogler have written about writing, on the craft of storytelling and the nature of myth. The theory goes that there's a story template of a "Hero's Journey": our hero begins in the ordinary world, then hears a call to adventure but refuses at first. A mentor helps our hero cross the threshold into a new world of adventure, where tests, allies, and enemies prove the mettle of his character. There's a supreme ordeal in the darkest of moments, but he comes through, revived, before returning home with a crucial reminder that this hasn't been a dream.

This story structure is there in *Harry Potter, Star Wars* (not the Holiday Special), even *Elf* and *Die Hard*. But it's also the story of Christmas. It began in an ordinary, unassuming Bethlehem, though the church at first refused the call to celebrate it. It took wise mentors like Emperor Constantine or St Nicholas of Myra to push Christmas over the threshold, where it was tested by kings, played with by mummers, and nearly killed off by Puritans. It saw us through the darkest moments of war, and came through the other side with tokens, symbols, and songs as reminders of the peace that it stands for.

In history's Nativity, Christmas has had shepherds like St Francis, three wise Victorian men in Irving, Dickens, and Albert, and choirs of angels including Bing Crosby, Joseph Mohr, and Reginald Fessenden.

As to where next for Christmas – well, Christmas doesn't know. It doesn't look forward, it looks back, just once a year. We still sum up our year in December, even if it's watching highlights of the year's news rather than counting our denarii or comparing our crops. And we'll keep harking back to a 2,000-year-old manger, via 1,000-year-old plays, 700-year-old carols, and a 500-year-old turkey – or possibly a twenty-year-old Japanese KFC Bargain Bucket.

However you celebrate, I know for certain that it's been said many times, in ways ranging from cards, crackers, films, and books to royal messages: but Merry Christmas to you. Oh and if it's not Christmas yet, I'm sure it will be soon. Because do you hear what I hear? Hark…

Bibliography

Still hungry? Put these on your Christmas list…

Benedict XVI, Pope. *Jesus of Nazareth: The Infancy Narratives.* Burns & Oates, 2012

Borg, Marcus J. & Crossan, John Dominic. *The First Christmas: What the Gospels Really Teach About Jesus' Birth.* HarperOne, 2009

Collins, Ace. *Stories Behind the Great Traditions of Christmas.* Zondervan, 2003

Collins, Ace. *Stories Behind the Best-Loved Songs of Christmas.* Zondervan, 2010

Connelly, Mark. *Christmas: A History.* I.B. Tauris, 2012

Count, Earl & Count, Alice. *4000 Years of Christmas: A Gift from the Ages.* Ulysses Press, 1997

Danes, Simon, ed. *A Christmas Anthology.* St Mark's Press, 2011

Daniel, Orville E. *A Harmony of the Four Gospels.* Baker Books, 1996

Douglas, Hugh. *A Right Royal Christmas.* The History Press, 2001

Dupont, Florence. *Daily Life in Ancient Rome.* Wiley-Blackwell, 1993

Eckstein, Bob. *The History of the Snowman.* Gallery Books, 2008

Hennessy, Brian. *Emergence of Broadcasting in Britain.* Southerleigh, 2005

Highfield, Roger. *Can Reindeer Fly?* Phoenix, 1998

Kernodle, George R. *The Theatre in History*. University of Arkansas Press, 1989

Luther, Martin. *Festival Sermons of Martin Luther*. Concordia Pub House, 2005

Macdonald, Fiona. *Christmas, A Very Peculiar History*. Book House, 2010

Miles, Clement A. *Christmas Customs and Traditions: Their History and Significance*. Dover, 1976

Roud, Steve. *The English Year*. Penguin, 2008

Rubin, Miri. *Mother of God: A History of the Virgin Mary*. Penguin, 2010

Struthers, Jane. *The Book of Christmas*. Ebury Press, 2012

Tydeman, William. *The Theatre in the Middle Ages: Western European Stage Conditions, c.800-1576*. Cambridge University Press, 2008

The Big Christmas Timeline

(ABRIDGED)

c. 4000 BC – Hunter-gatherers work with farmers to make so much food, they start the tradition of turkey leftovers (except no turkey)

c. 1500 BC – Scandinavian Bronze Age; Israelites go out for an Exodus, they may be some time

40 BC – Herod decreed "King of the Jews" by Rome… It won't last.

6 BC – Bright star spotted in Palestine. Definitely not a plane.

4 BC – Herod dies around now-ish, so Jesus is born around now-ish

AD 6 – Quirinius becomes Governor of Syria, and opening character for Nativity stories

135 – Emperor Hadrian builds a shrine to a Greek god over Jesus' birth-cave. Rude.

200 – Clement of Alexandria guesses Jesus' birthday, concluding definitely between 1 Jan and 31 Dec

270 – St Nicholas born in (ironically) Turkey, in a town named after (ironically) myrrh

274 – 25 December celebrated by… new official cult *solis invictus*. Join the queue, Christianity.

303 – Emperor Diocletian's Great Persecution of Christians. Not great.

313 – Christians get their things back

325 – Council of Nicaea, which is nice

336 – Happius Christmasus! Christmas celebrated in Rome by now

343 – St Nicholas dies on 6 December, which happens to be St Nicholas' Day

350 – Pope Julius I says he's looked into it: Jesus' birthday is 25 December

367 – New Testament exists; Matthew and Luke's accounts are in, Bartholomew's earthquake is out

380 – Christianity is the official religion of Rome, and the first proper Christmas decoration appears

529 – Emperor Justinian makes Christmas a civic holiday. Other Honda cars celebrate another time.

567 – Council of Tours decrees that there are *douze jours* of Christmas

597 – Towels at the ready… Augustine hosts mass Christmas Day baptism in Kent

601 – Pope Gregory tells Augustine, absorb don't replace (like the towels)

700 – 25 December celebrated across most of England. Cornwall will catch up dreckly.

800 – Charlemagne crowned Holy Roman Emperor on Christmas Day

935 – Good King Wenceslas dies. A very deep man. And crisp. And even.

1087 – St Nicholas' relics rehomed to Bari – which is a place in Italy, not a bloke

1100 – Baldwin of Boulogne crowned first king of Jerusalem in the Church of the Nativity in Bethlehem. Top that.

1171 – Roland the Farter entertains Henry II at Christmas by, well, the clue's in the name

1213 – King John eats A LOT at his birthday/Christmas feast

1223 – St Francis of Assisi pioneers the live Nativity. Arguably the first ever "Messy Church".

1248 – The poor fill Westminster Hall for Christmas Day dinner

1347 – First royal mummers play. Priests unsure. They should combine as a tribute band: "The Mummers & The Papists"...

1426 – All together now... English carol collection appears

1441 – First Christmas tree in a town square. And yes, it was set on fire.

1521 – Oh *that's* what they're saying... Christmas Mass in local language for first time

1525 – Turkeys arrive in Europe. Not for a holiday – sorry.

1526 – Nativity accounts in local languages, along with the rest of the Bible

1541 – Boy Bishop banned. All he did was dress up as the bishop...

1560 – McHumbug! Christmas banned in Scotland.

1604 – First American Christmas celebrated off the coast of Maine

1607 – King's players don't get Christmas Day off after all, as James I requests a Christmas play

1643 – Humbug! Puritans see who'll celebrate Christmas, and who won't.

1644 – Extra humbug! Christmas falls on a Sunday. Feast day or fast day? Dinner gets political.

1645 – Loads of humbug! No official Christmas in England; Parliament meets instead.

1646 – Humbu… Oof! Pro-Christmas and anti-Christmas protests.

1647 – The most amount of humbug! Christmas officially banned in England.

1658 – Plum Pudding Riots – though more dangerous than it sounds

1659 – "More than a feeling"? Boston bans Christmas

1660 – Gubmuh! Christmas returns to England

1670 – Candy canes created by Cologne Cathedral choirmaster

1700 – "While Shepherds Watched" distributed around England with the Book of Common Prayer

1717 – First pantomime in London. Oh no it isn't…

1742 – Handel debuts the long-awaited *Messiah*

1747 – Strike a light, it's the first Christingle service

1752 – Calendar change from Julian to Gregorian confuses when to celebrate Christmas

1800 – A German Christmas tree at Windsor; doesn't catch on

1804 – Hessian troops fell Christmas trees in Chicago. They get funny looks, but they're hard so don't care.

1809 – Washington Irving helps bring Sinterklaas to Americans

1818 – "Silent Night" debuts, thanks to some hungry mice, a tasty organ, and a last-minute poem

1819 – Washington Irving's *Sketch Book* reports on cosy English Christmas

1821 – Children's book features "Old Santeclaus"

1822 – Clement Clarke Moore writes "A Visit from St Nicholas"

1843 – *A Christmas Carol,* "O Come, All Ye Faithful", and the Christmas card all debut

1848 – "Once in Royal David's City" written; picture of royal Christmas tree spreads the custom

1857 – Oh what fun it is to write… "Jingle Bells" and "We Three Kings"

1862 – Macy's hosts first in-store Santa, and the first just-outside-store Santa, on his cigarette break

1864 – Brrr… First Christmas Day Hyde Park swim.

1871 – The workforce get Boxing Day off. I mean it's no twelve days…

1874 – Macy's first Christmas window display – window-shopping is born

1880 – The world's first Ninety Lessons and Carols service overruns due to a misprint

1882 – Edison employee Edward Johnson has a lightbulb moment: Christmas lights

1888 – "What do you want for Christmas? The first Santa's grotto, here in London? OK…"

1904 – *Peter Pan* debuts in London, believe it or not

1906 – Gather round the wireless – it's the first Christmas radio entertainment show

1908 – Advent calendars in, Christmas candle tree decorations out (say insurance companies)

The Big Christmas Timeline

1914 – Truce in the trenches

1915 – Santa drinks… Wait, White Rock ginger ale?

1918 – Lessons and Carols service in King's College, Cambridge

1922 – "This is London calling…" – first British Christmas radio broadcasts

1923 – First White House Christmas tree; first Christmas *Radio Times*

1931 – Santa drinks… Coke. Ho ho slurp.

1932 – One's first British royal Christmas message

1939 – *Rudolph the Red-Nosed Reindeer* is published, lighting the way for future songs

1941 – "White Christmas" debuts: May all your Christmas songs be as lucrative as this…

1958 – We don't need your Hogmanay, Hogmanay, Hogmanay… Scotland finally reinstates Christmas

1965 – "Jingle Bells" is the first song played in space, as part of a prank

1973 – Glam Wars: Slade vs Wizzard

1984 – Band Aid breaks records

1994 – Mariah Carey's "All I Want for Christmas is You" completes Christmas

2015 – Most online sales via mobile devices for the first time

2048 – Hologram of Bing Crosby hosts first Christmas singalong on Mars (TBC)

A Christmas Quiz!

(all answers within the book, or upside down on page 285)

1. Which climatic conditions inspired the writing of "Let It Snow! Let It Snow! Let It Snow!", "The Christmas Song", and "Sleigh Ride"?
a) A Baltimore blizzard b) A Hollywood heatwave c) A Manhattan monsoon

2. One letter-writing private at the 1914 Christmas Truce went on to write which animal-based book?
a) Fantastic Mr Fox *b)* Tarka the Otter *c)* Jeffrey the Weasel

3. What was the only new carol permitted by the Church of England in the 1700s?
a) "While Shepherds Watched Their Flocks" b) "Joy to the World" c) "Happy Christmas Cromwell"

4. According to Catholicism, who was conceived in "the immaculate conception"?
a) Jesus b) The shepherd girl c) Mary

5. Who are the only biblical characters to celebrate their own birthdays?
a) Noah and Judas b) Pharaoh and Herod c) Wise men #1 and #3

6. What featured on the first Christmas card in 1843?
a) A child drinking booze b) Prince Albert giving two thumbs up c) A crib scene with four wise men

7. Jester Roland Le Pettour was lured out of retirement by Henry II for what Christmas Day routine?
a) A leap, a whistle, and a fart b) Juggling hedgehogs c) "I hope my tunic doesn't catch fire…"

8. What did Chicago locals look at, bemused, in December 1804?
a) Norwegian farmers' briefly flying reindeer b) German soldiers felling fir trees c) Russian chefs' impromptu ballet-dancing

9. Which of these was Christmas NOT called in England in the 1640s?
a) Boxing Eve b) The Profane Man's Ranting Day c) The Multitudes' Idle Day

10. Which of these was the original spelling of a reindeer's name from Clement Clarke Moore's poem "A Visit from St Nicholas"?
a) Dunder b) Flitzen c) Thrasher

11. Candlemas is otherwise known as what?
a) The Day of the Triffids *b)* Groundhog Day *c)* The Day the Earth Stood Still

12. The composer of "Little Donkey" also wrote which other animal-based song?
a) "Ox and Ass and Gerbil" b) "One More Sheep till Christmas" c) "I've Got a Little Whippet"

13. In what Christmassy-sounding place was St Nicholas born?
a) Bethlehemville b) Turkey c) Caracas

14. What Christmassy substance was said to emanate from St Nicholas' bones?
a) Gold b) Frankincense c) Myrrh

15. Which one of these song facts is NOT true?
a) "Jingle Bells" was the first song in space, as part of a Santa/alien prank
b) "White Christmas" was the warning alarm for US troops to leave Saigon
c) "Silent Night" was the first song to top the charts in Klingon

16. Washington Irving is responsible for popularizing Santa Claus in North America – and what else?
a) Robinson Crusoe *and the word "pants"*
b) Rip Van Winkle *and the word "knickers"*
c) Rupert the Bear *and the word "stockings"*

17. Which of these was NOT the name of one of King Herod's wives?
a) Herodia b) Cleopatra c) Doris

18. What's the customary Japanese Christmas dinner?
a) Burger King b) KFC c) McDonald's

19. The poinsettia plant is named after whom or where?
a) A school in Poinse, New Jersey
b) Dr Joel Poinsett, first US Minister to Mexico
c) Edgar Allen Poe, in Seattle

20. What's the traditional response to "Wassail!"?
a) "Who's there?" b) "Wassail who?" c) "Drinkhail!"

ANSWERS below!

1 b). 2 b). 3 a). 4 c). 5 b). 6 a). 7 a). 8 b). 9 a). 10 a). 11 b). 12 c). 13 b). 14 c). 15 c). 16 b). 17 a). 18 b). 19 b). 20 c).

P.S. Wishing you a very:

Merry Christmas!